HOW TO SELL YOUR HOME

How to Sell Your Home

The essential guide to a fast, stress-free, and profitable sale

MINDY JENSEN

BiggerPockets® PUBLISHING

How to Sell Your Home

Mindy Jensen

Published by BiggerPockets Publishing LLC, Denver, CO

Copyright © 2018 by Mindy Jensen.

All Rights Reserved.

Publisher's Cataloging-in-Publication data

Names: Jensen, Mindy Sue., author.

Title: How to sell your home : the essential guide to a fast , stress-free , and profitable sale /

Mindy Jensen.

Description: Denver, CO : BiggerPockets Pub., 2018.

Identifiers: ISBN 9780997584738 (pbk.) | 978-0-9975847-4-5 (ebook) | LCCN 2017953887

Subjects: LCSH House selling. | Real estate business. | Home ownership. | BISAC BUSINESS & ECONOMICS / Real Estate / Buying & Selling Homes

Classification: LCC HD1379 .J45 2018 | DDC 643/.12--dc23

Printed in the United States of America

10 9 8 7 6 5 4 3 2 1

Dedication

For Carl, because I would not be what I am today without you.
For Claire and Daphne, because you're my world.

And for my parents, who showed me that
moving really isn't that hard.

Contents

Preface

You're considering selling your home. This is a huge decision. You may have lived in the home for many years and grown very attached to it. Perhaps your children took their first steps in the home or figured out how to ride a bike down your street.

In a hot market, the home-sale process could be as easy as listing your house, having a handful of showings, and trying to decide which of the many offers—and at what terms—you should accept. You are in control of the entire process, and buyers will do almost anything for the privilege of buying your home.

In a cold market, the experience is very different and could entail a lot of sitting around and waiting, getting your hopes up during every showing, and being very disappointed when no offer comes through. You are at the mercy of any buyer who comes along, especially if you *have* to sell. There are still many markets that fall into this category, unfortunately.

Unless you buy and sell homes every day, you may be surprised at what pops up during the course of a sale—from inspection issues to appraisal problems to last-minute mortgage denials. A sale isn't sold until everyone signs everything and the money changes hands.

You will always encounter surprises.

No two home sales are alike: no two buyers, no two sellers, and certainly no two houses. While every sale is different, there are consistent elements in every residential real estate transaction. There is always a property, a buyer, and a seller. Here, you are the seller.

If you've never sold a house before, you are in for an adventure. While it would be nice if you just listed your home and someone handed you a giant pile of cash and it was sold, that isn't how it works. There's a lot more to it than that!

If you have sold a house but it's been a while since you went through the steps, you'll find that things have changed. A lot! There are new laws and regulations, new procedures, and even new types of loans your buyer may be using—and not every loan is created equal.

But never fear, dear reader. I have sold houses and sold them recently. I've been through the changes, and I will hold your hand throughout the entire experience. I will outline the most common scenarios you may encounter during your sale to help you arrive at the closing table with as few surprises as possible.

ABOUT ME

I'm a licensed real estate agent in Colorado. In addition to helping people buy and sell their homes, I've been investing in real estate for almost 20 years. I've flipped eight homes and owned a few rental properties. I love everything about real estate and love teaching others. In fact, I work at BiggerPockets, the number one company in real estate investment education. As the community manager for BiggerPockets, I talk to real estate investors all day long. I'm entrenched in my local real estate market, and my contacts with investors across the United States have given me a great understanding about many other markets across the country.

I've sold houses in many different types of markets. This book is for anyone who needs to sell his or her home but isn't quite sure how to get that accomplished. If you've never sold a home, you might be surprised at everything you need to do. It's not difficult, but if you miss a step, you could put your sale in jeopardy.

As a homeowner, it's easy to get overwhelmed. Selling your home involves more than just putting a sign in the front yard. If you've lived in the home for a long time, you're going to need to get it ready to show before you can allow people in. I'll share tips from my personal experiences as well as mistakes I've seen homeowners make.

If you're an investor, your road is a little different because you likely have not lived in the home. It may be a rental you've owned for years or a home you just bought, fixed up, and are now selling for a tidy profit. Now that you're in the home stretch, it might make sense to try to sell it yourself instead of hiring an agent. Or it might not.

I'll address all these subjects and more!

TRUE LIFE STORY

Throughout the book, I've included stories drawn mostly from my own experiences with selling homes. While some of those endeavors were personally painful, I hope that they will help you avoid some issues I have lived through. After all, experience really is the best teacher.

PRO·TIP *I've also included tips in every chapter to drive home the key points to remember in the selling process.*

CHAPTER 1
Introduction

You want to sell your house, or you're at least considering it. Whether you're moving for a job transfer, to upsize or downsize, or because you just can't stand to live in your current house for another minute, you need to follow the right path to get the most money for your home. But money isn't the only consideration. You also need to sell in a time frame that works best for you and have a smooth transition to your next house.

There's a lot more to it than just planting a sign in the front yard.

This is likely one of the biggest transactions of your life and you don't want to make any mistakes! In fact, you've got a lot of work ahead of you before you can even *think* about putting it on the market and start accepting showings.

First, you have to decide whether you want to find an agent or sell your home yourself. Sure, it would be awesome to be able to save yourself the commission, but is that the best choice for your needs? Do you know the right questions to ask of potential agents to help you find the best person to represent you and your interests?

Rehabbing your property may result in a higher offer, but what should you concentrate on when fixing it up? How much should you spend to get your home in show condition? What repairs or improvements just aren't worth your time and money?

More questions: How fast will it sell? This depends on what type of market you're in. A buyer's market means there are more properties than there are buyers and homes are typically undervalued in this type of market. The buyers you do attract want a deal, and getting your house sold can take a really long time. On the other hand, a seller's market means there are more people buying than there are properties for sale. Prices go up, buyer demands go down, and selling is a breeze.

Then come the offers: Once you have an offer, how do you know it's a good one? If you've received multiple offers, how do you choose the best? What makes one offer better than another? The highest offer can seem really nice—and a no-brainer to accept—but another offer may have terms that work better for you. Sometimes that high offer isn't really that high when you take into consideration the concessions (the money or credit you're giving to the buyer for closing costs, buying points for their loans, and so on) the offer is requesting.

Guess what. There are also tons of fees: Do you know all the costs associated with selling a house in your city, county, and state? Some cities have transfer taxes. Closing costs include more than just title insurance, agent commissions, and attorney fees. Selling your house is going to cost you money. Period. Do you have enough equity in the property to make it worth your while? If you just *want* to sell—rather than *need* to sell—it may make more financial sense to wait for a better market. If you *have* to sell and have little equity, you may need to bring money to the closing table, meaning you may have to write a check to sell your home.

The questions you need to address are endless.

Are you mentally ready to keep your home in neat, show condition for the next thirty, sixty, or ninety-plus days? Where are you going to move? Have you found your new house yet? Are you in such a slow market that selling is going to take a long time?

How much are you willing to address if the home inspection discovers things that need to be repaired? Do you want to coordinate the repairs yourself or give a credit to the buyers so they can take care of the repairs?

What do you do if the property does not appraise at the offer price? What happens if the buyers change their mind? What if they cannot get financing or their funding falls through at the last minute? What if they simply walk away?

Reality check: Is it even worth selling? If you're in a down market, think of the bottom line. Would renting out your home while you wait for a more favorable selling season benefit you?

Finally, when you do close, what does all that legal jargon mean? What does closing even mean?

I'll answer all these questions—and more—so you can have the best possible experience while selling your current house and moving in to your next home. This book will help you make it to the closing table with no surprises. We'll walk through the process of both a smooth sale and a not-so-smooth sale, so you can be as prepared as possible for any situation your home sale may turn up.

While this book is geared toward homeowners who want to sell their house, if you're an investor, there is still plenty to learn from the tips in this book—especially if you've never sold a house before! There's more to it than just planting a sign in the front yard.

CHAPTER 2

Decisions in Selling

You're thinking about selling your home. That's why you picked up this book.

WHAT IS YOUR WHY?

For many people, a home represents much more than just a place to hang their hat. There are emotions involved after all, especially if you've made some wonderful memories there. For most of us, choosing to sell is a monumental decision. Knowing your why will help you make the best choices during the selling process. Why do you need to sell your home?

Accepting a job thousands of miles across the country is a great *need* to sell. Viewing a positive pregnancy test result while living in a one-bedroom condo is also a really great need to sell. Perhaps you and your new spouse are Brady-Bunching it and have a large family to accommodate.

Or you might be on the other end of the spectrum: Your kids have all moved out, and now the house is just too big for you.

Or maybe you simply hate your home. It has an ugly kitchen, or the neighborhood has changed since you first moved in. Perhaps you've simply fallen out of love with the whole thing. Not wanting to live in the house any longer can make you yearn for greener pastures.

Whatever your reason to sell, it is valid. Valid, however, does not equal urgent, and some reasons for selling are more urgent than others.

Some of the most common reasons for selling a house are:

- Job transfer
- Upsizing—the house is too small
- Downsizing—the house is too big
- Cashing in on equity
- Marriage
- Divorce
- Declining health

 Stop and take a moment now to consider why you are selling. This has an effect on your decision making further into the sales process.

WANT VERSUS NEED

Living in a small home—like that one-bedroom condo we talked about earlier—and then going to an ultrasound to discover that you are expecting triplets will present a more urgent sales need than simply being sick of your kitchen.

Your urgency coupled with your reason for selling will direct your sales path. Accepting a lowball offer in a buyer's market is a lot easier when you *need* to sell. Waiting for a better offer—or a better market— is much easier to do when you just *want* to sell.

There are two factors to selling: Determining *why* you want to sell and figuring out *how fast* you need to sell. These factors enable you to make the best choices during the sales process. The *why* and *how fast* are the two factors that influence every aspect of your sale, from the price at which you list the property and how aggressively you market it to the type of offer you accept. These factors will also affect how you deal with inspection issues, time of possession, and closing. Indeed, the amount you pocket from the sale is tied directly to your need to sell. You are far less likely to take a low offer if the reason you are selling is simply because you *want* to. Being sick of your kitchen won't compel you to take an offer deeply under asking price. Conversely when nobody seems to want to buy your house, but the due date for those triplets is fast approaching, that low offer that finally comes in may suddenly seem very appealing.

Take some time to determine need versus want while considering your desired timeline for a sale and the drop-dead date you need to be out. Are there any alternatives to selling? Could you turn home into a rental? Could simply remodeling your current space be an option for you?

You've determined your why. You have both an ideal timeline as well as a drop-dead deadline to be out of the home. You are prepared to sever all ties with this property and move on to the next chapter of your life. Let's get started!

CHAPTER 3
The Investor Introduction

For the investor, selling a property has similar but different challenges as the ones facing an owner-occupant seller (someone who lives in the home and is selling it because he or she is moving out). If you're a landlord, you must decide whether you want to sell the property with your tenants in place or try to sell it vacant. Selling with tenants in place requires some finesse, while selling vacant requires you to foot all the incoming bills until the property sells. Your tenant may be the entire reason you're selling. If you have a difficult tenant, like one who isn't paying or one who will most likely be evicted, be honest and upfront with your potential buyer. There is a buyer for every situation.

Depending on the type of property you're selling, you may be selling to another investor. Gather up your numbers and data about the property because he or she is going to ask for them. If you've recently rehabbed the home, you're most likely selling to owner-occupant buyers. Your path will mirror that of an owner-occupant seller detailed in this book.

SELLING AS A LANDLORD

Selling a house as a landlord requires the same basics steps as those an owner-occupant seller would follow. You still have to prepare the property for showings, but you will need to coordinate with your tenants' schedules first and fully communicate your intent.

Occupied properties

Selling a property with tenants in place allows you to continue to collect rent checks during the sales process. The best-case scenario is that you sell to another landlord, who simply steps into your shoes and takes over existing leases.

You'll need to find all the documents you have for the property. Gather together proof of any repairs or upgrades made while you were the owner. Collect documents pertaining to the tenants themselves: all leases and addendums, background checks that you obtained during tenant screening, tenant estoppel letters, which comes from the tenants and documents their monthly rent, how much of a security deposit they paid, when the rent is due, and so on. Make sure you double-check these files against the records you have and resolve all discrepancies before you put the house on the market. Also include a history of rent payments to show a pattern of when you received rent from the tenants.

Communicate with your tenants before you put the house on the market. Tell them you're thinking of selling, and find out whether they might want to buy it themselves. (How awesome would it be to just skip the whole "finding a buyer" thing if you already have one living in the house?)

If they're not going to buy the house, ask them their preferred times for showing. Encourage your tenants to not be present during showings. While you're meeting with them, look around the property to gauge the condition of the home. Remember, this is how buyers will see the property too.

If you performed a walk-through of the property before the tenants took possession, prepare to share that document with the new owners. Consider scheduling a walk-through prior to closing. Invite the tenants to be present so they can be up-front with the new owner about the property, and the new owner has an even stronger sense of security about purchasing it. You may also want the agent to schedule showings with the tenant rather than with you, as long as the tenant does not deny too many showings.

Be truthful with potential buyers. If you're selling because you're tired of dealing with bad tenants, share your concerns with them. The golden rule applies in real estate, and there truly is a buyer for every property. You wouldn't want to purchase a property without knowing about a problem tenant, right? Don't do that to your buyer either.

Tenant information will need to be included in the disclosures. We will discuss disclosures later in this book, so prepare to document issues you've had with your tenants. Additionally, the lease is for the property, not the landlord. Note in your listing the month the current lease ends, whether the current tenants are on a month-to-month lease, the amount of rent paid each month, and their desire to stay or leave upon the lease's end.

Unoccupied properties
Selling an unoccupied property may sound easier because there is no tenant to coordinate showings with and no worrying about the condition of the property. However, if you don't have a tenant in place, the costs fall onto your shoulders. You need to pay the utilities, mortgage, insurance, and cover any repairs needed until the property sells. You'll also want to stage the property with furniture.

SELLING AS A FLIPPER
If you bought a property, rehabbed it, and are now selling it a short time later, your process is very similar to that of an owner-occupied home. You're most likely not selling to another investor, so you will also want to stage the home to help buyers to fully visualize your rehab work. Staging means putting furniture into the home to "set the stage" and give buyers an idea of how to use the space. If the home has any oddly shaped spaces or if there is a question about what to do with a room, stage it. Buyers can probably figure out the best use for a bedroom but that weird space in the hallway may be tough for them to visualize. If you make it clear to buyers what they can do with the space, you will succeed in making them want to buy your property.

You should also prepare a list of repairs and upgrades that have been performed on the property in your rehab. This list should be printed out, framed, and prominently displayed in the kitchen, with other information about the home. You want people to not only know you've done the work but also see the scope of the work so they understand the asking price. Be sure to highlight unseen upgrades, such as electrical or plumbing, and point out anything that comes with a transferable warranty. Finally, include all the service manuals for new appliances you've added, along with a list of upgrades. Note the date these upgrades were performed, and place everything in a binder.

Owner-occupant sellers will fill out a seller's property disclosure form, and as a house flipper, you should fill this out too. While you haven't lived in the property, you should still know about its condition. Be honest in your disclosure! Understand that there is a buyer for every property in any condition, and disclosures are designed to protect you. You'll learn more about disclosure in chapter eight.

CHAPTER 4

Buyer's Market versus Seller's Market

You may have heard the terms *buyer's market* and *seller's market* in the news regarding the general housing market in your area. The specific type of market you are in is determined by how many homes are on the market (the inventory)—and how fast they're selling. Inventory refers to the numbers of houses for sale in a certain market at any given time. Inventory levels determine whether your area is a buyer's market or a seller's market. Let's say you have 4,000 houses on the market, and homes are selling at a rate of 1,000 per month. This means that there are four months of inventory on the market because the number of available houses (4,000) divided by the current selling rate (1,000) equals four.

BUYER'S MARKET

A buyer's market is one in which there are more people selling their homes than there are people looking to buy. The buyers have their pick of properties, and sellers need their houses to be top-notch for buyers to even come look at the home. A buyer's market happens when there is more than six months' worth of inventory on the market.

Prices are low in a buyer's market, and properties sell slowly. Sellers have very little room to negotiate because buyers will simply move on to the next property. Contingencies are numerous: For instance, buyers will request every issue found during the home inspection to be repaired before closing and may ask for help with closing costs, something known as seller concessions.

In a buyer's market, sellers are at the mercy of the buyers they are hoping to attract. When you're trying to sell your home, a buyer's market makes it much more difficult and is definitely *not* a favorable market for you.

The good news is that a buyer's market does not last forever. The pendulum will eventually swing back toward a more balanced or even seller-favorable market if you just give it some time. If your urgency to sell is low and you find yourself in a buyer's market, you may consider waiting to list your home or even renting it out until the local market conditions change.

SELLER'S MARKET

A seller's market, on the other hand, is one in which there are more people buying houses than there are people selling them. Buyers have to take what they can get, and sellers can refuse buyer requests for things like repairs or concessions at closing. They can even dictate the terms under which they will vacate the property. When you're selling your home, a seller's market is ideal—that is, unless you then must turn around and buy another home in the area. A seller's market happens when there is less than three months' worth of inventory on the market.

 Ask your agent about the current market conditions and how much inventory is on the market.

Cash offers are common, contingencies are few, if any, and receiving multiple offers on your home is expected. Buyers in these markets have a much more difficult time getting their offer accepted and frequently will start their offer at or above asking price.

During the housing downturn of 2007 to 2012, home builders stopped building. In fact, many went out of business and found different professions altogether. Five-plus years of very few newly built homes turned into quite a deficit of available housing, especially in areas of the country where the population was growing. The laws of supply and demand kicked in and forced prices up. If you are selling your home in a seller's market and want to upgrade to a new house, make sure you can actually find a home to buy before listing your own.

BALANCED MARKET

Markets aren't just buyer's or seller's markets. Sometimes there is a balance when buyers and sellers have healthy (but not too much) competition. A balanced market occurs when there is between three and six months' worth of inventory on the market.

Properties stay on the market for a decent amount of time—but there isn't the frenzy of a seller's market or the desperation of a buyer's market. There is a much more relaxed, normal feel to the market and to the entire process.

DETERMINING YOUR MARKET

Knowing what market you're in can help you craft your sale and determine if now is the best time to sell. Markets don't last forever, and there is a lot of fluctuation: A buyer's market will eventually become more balanced or change direction completely.

If you're using a real estate agent to help you sell your home, ask him or her whether you're in a buyer's, seller's, or balanced market. Ask for the average number of days on the market and the difference between selling price and asking price of recently sold homes.

CHAPTER 5

Getting Sale Ready, Part One: Repairs

When you've lived in your home for a while, you know everything about it. But you aren't trying to sell it to yourself, which means you need to convince someone new that they cannot live without this house. You may love the pink carpeting you installed or that wallpaper with clowns that you painstakingly hung, but remember that your tastes may not reflect those of the general populace. Accept this, and don't take it personally: It's now time to look at your home from a completely different perspective.

You need to present your home in the best possible light and want it as close to perfect as you can get. This means fixing up all those little—and not so little—things you've been living with during your time in the home. Including that clown wallpaper. Yes, clown wallpaper.

TRUE LIFE STORY

I once showed a home that had clown wallpaper not only on every wall but also on the ceiling! Yikes! Like all truly ugly wallpaper, it was glued on with the strongest, most difficult-to-remove wallpaper glue ever invented. To be honest, the rest of the house wasn't amazing either. It had very ugly tile, even uglier cabinets in the kitchen, and pink marble slab around the fireplace. The clowns were the least of the concerns. My clients made a lowball offer that was not accepted by the seller, who eventually ended up selling several months later for less than what my clients had offered because the listing had long since gone stale.

MAKE REPAIRS NOW

In every house, there are things that need to be jiggled this way or nudged that way for them to work properly. For example, in my own home, I have to lift the door handle up to get the door to lock. This is obviously not a deal breaker, but it is an annoyance.

The problem is, if your home has too many of these annoyances, they start to become deal breakers, with potential buyers thinking, "What other annoying things am I going to find after I move in?"

I'm a licensed agent in Colorado, and during showings, it's inevitable that I come across a door that will not open. Real estate agents probably open more doors than the rest of the human race combined, and if *they* can't get the door to unlock, you've got a problem. If your front door is off-kilter, fix it before the home goes on the market.

PRO·TIP *Nobody is going to buy your house if he or she can't even get in the front door!*

It doesn't stop at the front door. Say to yourself, "Does the toilet wobble when I sit on it? Is there a light switch that is fussy?" Do you have an outlet that simply does not work? Just because you've been living with it doesn't mean someone else will want to. Right now—before the house is listed for sale—is the time to fix all those little things you've been dealing with, so make a list, break out your toolbox, and get to work.

PRO·TIP *Schedule enough time to do each job correctly. Tasks always take twice as long as you think.*

Not handy? Go through the entire house room by room and make a list of every single thing that isn't quite right and then contact a handyman. Actually, contact three or four of them and get quotes from each for comparison shopping. Consider having a handyman come out and go over the jobs with you so can you get an accurate measure of the time and cost involved. Yes, it's going to cost you money out of pocket that you don't want to spend on a home you will no longer living in, but this will help you sell your house. It's going to cost money to sell your house. And yes, that stinks. But you either pay it up front or at the end in the form of a lower offer price.

The closer to perfection your home is, the fewer objections your buyer will have and the higher the initial offer will be. The buyer will have fewer repair requests after the inspection, and your house will sell more easily. Again, do something about that clown wallpaper.

FRESHEN THE INTERIOR

When the repairs are complete, walk through the entire home again and look for anything that's worn, outdated, broken, dingy, or dirty. Look closely!

Do you have outlet covers that are broken, cracked, or missing? Do you have any custom outlet covers that you want to take with you? Swap those out for regular covers before the home goes on the market.

Buyers can't request that you leave something in the home if they haven't even seen it. If it's special to you, don't take the chance that the buyer will also fall in love with it and want it!

Do you have children? Those small hands touch the same spots on the walls and trim over and over, leaving marks. Consider painting the rooms or pieces of trim that look dirty or dingy. Traffic patterns are worn into carpeting over time. Check out the carpet in high traffic areas for discoloration or staining. A lot of traffic occurs around interior doors. If fresh paint and new carpet aren't in the budget, wipe down the walls and steam clean the carpets for a quick pick-me-up.

Look at the ceilings. Clear out cobwebs, wipe down the blades of the ceiling fans, and clear out the dust and dead insects in the light fixtures. What about those light fixtures? An older but clean light fixture looks better than an older but dirty one. How old is the light fixture? Changing outdated fixtures can give a room an entirely different look. There isn't a rule of thumb about what constitutes outdated, but you can easily compare styles to what's currently being sold in stores. Brass light fixtures from the 1980s can make a home look like it's stuck in the past. If all-new light fixtures aren't in your budget, consider at least installing a new one to draw a buyer's attention to the main living space or the kitchen.

Look closely at the floors. Do your hardwood floors have gouges, scuffs, and scrapes? Are there any cracked or dirty tiles? What about missing grout? Does the linoleum have any holes or damage? Is your carpet stained and matted? Anything that can be repaired quickly or for little out-of-pocket expense should be fixed before the home goes on the market. Depending on your financial situation, a small outlay of cash now can net you a higher offer—and put more money into your pocket at closing. Again, at the very least, it should be clean. Rent a steam cleaner and put it to work.

Smell your home. Every house has a scent, and your house is no different. In fact, your smell is probably unique and you likely can't smell your own home. You've lived in it for too long and are too used to it or just don't notice it. Make no mistake, your buyers will notice it. Not all home aromas are unpleasant, but if you've got animals, they've likely contributed their own scent too. Many pet owners are unaware of what their home smells like to others. If you have animals and carpet, you could have an odor problem. If you have animals that use a litter box, you could have an odor problem. If time is an issue, consider hiring a cleaning service to come in and give the house a top-to-bottom deep cleaning. Tell the service you're putting the house on the market and you want it to sparkle. A few hundred dollars in professional cleaning costs can be easily recouped by the higher selling price that a fresh, clean home garners.

TRUE LIFE STORY

I once showed a house to clients, and as soon as I opened the door, I was slapped in the face with a sickly sweet wall of scent from a room freshener. The problem with a cover-up room freshener is that the underlying problem has usually not been addressed, and it's easy to detect the pet smell beneath the perfume—or at least wonder what the underlying problem is.

Do you smoke in your house? Right now is the time to stop smoking inside and air the house out. If you've smoked inside the house for an extended period of time, there may be nicotine stains on the wall. A fifty:fifty mix of water-to-vinegar solution is very effective at removing nicotine from walls, but note that this will take a lot of elbow grease.

PRO·TIP *Place charcoal on plates, or white vinegar in dishes, around the house to absorb the smoke smell.*

Ask a good friend to come over and tell you honestly what your home smells like. If he or she says anything other than "Fresh as a daisy!" then you have an issue. An ozonator is a great start, and you can rent or buy one from your local home improvement store.

Clean is better than dirty, but brand-new beats it all.

INTERIOR FRESHEN CHECKLIST:

- ☐ Anything that is worn, outdated, broken, dingy, or dirty
- ☐ Outlet covers
- ☐ Trim and walls
- ☐ Carpet, especially in high-traffic areas
- ☐ Ceilings, light fixtures, fans
- ☐ Floors: linoleum, hardwood, carpet
- ☐ Smells

FRESHEN THE EXTERIOR

After you have repaired everything on the inside of the home, step outside and make sure the exterior looks amazing too.

PRO·TIP *Curb appeal is real. You never get a second chance to make a first impression.*

Buyers may choose not to even see the inside of your home if the outside is a complete disaster. This has happened to me: I once drove clients to a house, and they didn't even want to get out of the car based just on the exterior of the property. In today's digital age, potential buyers have most likely seen your home before their agent has made the showing appointment, but none of that matters if they won't even get out of the car in person.

No matter what time of year your house is on the market, the exterior can and should still look nice. Paint is just about the only thing you cannot do during the bitter cold winter months. If your home needs a paint job—and it is just too darn cold—the rest of the outside had better make up for the paint.

In autumn, every leaf should be picked up. Old, dead plant stems should be cut back in preparation for the spring months. Spray weed killer so weeds like crabgrass and dandelions aren't visible. Trees and bushes should be trimmed or hedged cleanly. Grass should be edged and not dead, dying, or brown. Rocks should be in their correct place in the landscaping. If they've been kicked out of their spots, put them back. It should go without saying that any pet waste should be removed and properly disposed of. Your kids' toys should be neatly placed in the garage and not strewn about the lawn.

In the spring and summer months, all of the above still applies, but your exterior should be clean, painted if necessary, and foliage should be planted. I use a variety of annual and perennial flowers in my own yard, and any annuals you used last year should be replanted for this year. The grass should be mowed every week and the trimmings picked up.

When was the last time you cleaned out your gutters? What is the condition of your landscaping lights? Do your exterior light fixtures make your home look dated? Are they clean and free of cobwebs and bugs? Are your deck railings nice and tight, or do they wiggle when you hold on to them? Does the sliding glass door roll smoothly, or is it difficult to open? Are your windows and screens clean and clear? Where is your garbage can sitting, and how smelly is it?

PRO·TIP *The exterior of the house itself should be sparkling, but please note that power washing is not a do-it-yourself project, unless you have done it before. Hire this job out if your home is dirty—and make sure you get someone with experience! A power washer can very easily take paint off siding, and the pennies you'll save by doing it yourself will be easily swallowed up by the cost of an entirely new exterior paint job.*

Not everyone will be viewing your home during the daytime. Have your landscaping looking great at night to appeal to those evening showings too. Landscape lights are cheap and easy to install. Get a bright light that shines on your house address numbers to make finding your home after dark easier. Any hanging baskets or other landscape features you'd like to highlight should have lights aimed at them as well.

You want your home to look so good that people drive up and scramble to get out of the car. Pay attention to the little things like the mailbox, house address numbers, light fixtures, and planters. A bold-colored front door will give a punch for very little expense. Fresh flowers, planters, new paint, and clean windows and doors all invite people to come inside.

DO YOU NEED REHAB?

I have read numerous "Which Renovation Projects Give You the Most Return on Investment?" articles. They all say the same basic thing: You're not going to get back all that you put into the rehab.

The top return on investment I read about was 90 percent, and that was for a minor kitchen remodel under $15,000. In simple math terms, if you spend $15,000 on a minor remodel, which is practically nothing when it comes to kitchens, you will earn yourself an additional $13,500 in the offer. You're losing money on this rehab! I'm not saying you shouldn't do anything to fix up your house. You should absolutely repair broken items—or note them on the property disclosure form, which I'll get to later—but now is not the time to undertake large rehab projects.

If you have a lime-green kitchen, investing in a $35 gallon of neutral-colored paint is going to pay back in spades! If you've decorated your kids' rooms with cartoon-character wallpaper or a fancy mural, take down the wallpaper and paint over the mural with a soft blue or green while attempting to ignore your children's tears. But a brand-new kitchen or bathroom? I'd pass—the investment isn't worth your time. Also, the money spent on the project will not be recouped, and living through a rehab is frustrating, especially when you won't benefit from the updates. What if you did all that work and then discovered that after closing, the new owners ripped out the kitchen and put in their own?

PRO·TIP *Place vinyl sheeting on the bottom of the cabinet under the sink—it's a quick fix and hides really gross stains that always seem to accumulate there.*

CHAPTER 6

Getting Sale Ready, Part Two: Declutter

Your home has too much stuff in it. No, I'm not peeking through your windows and spying on you—I've just seen *a lot* of homes in every shape, size, and state of disarray. Don't feel bad. My house has way too much stuff in it, too, but the difference between you and me is that I'm not selling my house.

Decluttering helps you in two ways: First, it showcases the house itself instead of your supercool snow globe collection or your awesome assortment of beer cans from around the world. Personal trinkets are great, but they're just that: personal. That isn't what people are buying. Buyers need to distinguish the actual house from your things inside it. Don't confuse your buyers with clutter, trinkets, and collections that aren't relevant to the sale.

Double win: Decluttering also gives you a head start on packing. Your home will soon be someone else's, and you're completely moving out when you sell it. There is no need for you to leave anything behind, so why wait until you get an offer to start packing up the things you don't need?

Start in the closets. Pack up out-of-season clothes and shoes, extra blankets and linens, books you won't read in the next six months, extra utensils and dishes, that turkey pan you use only once a year (unless you're selling during turkey season), and toys your kids don't really need. Take this time to evaluate how necessary these items are. Take usable items to the local thrift store so someone else can benefit from them—and so you won't have to move them or unpack them at your next house. Anything that's dusty isn't being used. Donate or toss.

Anything you haven't used in two months isn't something you need. Donate or toss.

Remove almost anything that is personal. Your goal is to have potential buyers see themselves in the home, and your personal items detract from the picture you want them to build in their mind. Your cute kids' pictures should be packed away, replaced by generic and boring images of landscapes and otherwise nonpersonal imagery.

TIDY CLOSETS AND CABINETS

Clutter makes a home look smaller than it is. You may be tempted to hide things in closets, drawers, or cabinets, thinking that will make your house look clean. But don't do this. Serious home buyers are opening everything, including dresser drawers that aren't even being sold with the house!

News flash: You're selling your house. Before you put it on the market, clean out the closets. You want them to look cavernous, not crammed and undersized.

TRUE LIFE STORY

I once bought a house with the intention of remodeling it, so I didn't care what the closets looked like. The previous occupant was obsessed with clothing. She had five closets, all the size of a hallway coat closet, so jam-packed with clothes that I didn't know how she was even able to take things out or put more things in. It definitely did not look spacious, but I still purchased the house with a vision beyond packed closets in mind.

This same idea goes for kitchens and bathrooms. Plan on every single cabinet and every single drawer being opened. To make the spaces inside look larger, remove anything that isn't vital to your life, and remove doubles or triples of utensils. Will you *really* need that potato masher or egg slicer in the next three months? Let's be honest: Do you really need it at all? How many wooden spoons do you use in the course of preparing a meal? Minimize your stuff!

Make meal plans based on the contents of the cabinets so you can be sure to use up food items before you have to move them. Find a fun recipe that requires that year-old container of oats. Clear out your spice cabinet and get rid of old jars. If you have small children, your refrigerator is probably covered in artwork, but a home shows better without the clutter. Save the art in a file folder and break it out in your next home. A couple of magnets on the refrigerator are fine, but anything else should be packed away.

In the bathroom, toss those shampoo and lotion bottles with less than an inch left at the bottom. The same goes for that perfume you never wear, those samples you aren't using, and every single bar of hotel soap you have collected. Better yet, contact your local homeless or women's shelter—they can use those small bars of soap. Clear out and properly dispose of any out-of-date medications and cosmetics. Ditch old toothbrushes and toothpaste. Do you have a junk drawer? Basically, just toss out everything in it and make your life easy.

Having items jammed into cabinets only makes the home look small and gives the impression of not having enough storage space— and storage space is a huge seller. You need to make your cabinets tidy and appear more spacious, so now is not the time to stock up on sale items or shop at bulk-purchase price clubs.

How much large furniture do you own? If you have more than two couches in a room, remove the extras. Either put them in a storage facility or, at the very least, move them out to the garage. If you can swing it, a storage facility will work even better because you'll be able to give buyers the impression of a home with plenty of room. Storing extra things like couches in the garage can make your house seem as if there is not enough space for all the necessities.

Can you move easily from room to room with the furniture in its current place, or do you need to twist your body or walk in an unnatural pattern to get around the home? If potential buyers walk into your home and your furniture is so overwhelming that they can't see past it, you've just lost a sale.

PRO·TIP   *Remember, you want buyers to be able to picture their own lives in your home so they will buy it.*

BASEMENTS AND ATTICS

Remember the house with all the tiny closets packed with clothes? That same house also had an attic. The woman I bought the home from lived there her entire life—her grandparents had built it and she grew up there, so I'm sure you can imagine the stuff that had accumulated in the space over the course of 50 years. Top to bottom, side to side, the entire attic was stuffed with things that someone neither wanted nor wanted to throw away. In fact, I was so wary of the seller's leaving something in the attic, I actually wrote into the contract that all personal effects needed to be removed from the home before closing.

If you are in a red-hot market, buyers are going to care a lot less about your stipulations. But if your market is slow, you want to give potential buyers every reason to write a contract for your home. You do not want to make it easy for them to pass on your home and explore other options.

PRO·TIP   *Uncluttered, open, spacious-looking houses sell faster in any market.*

USE STORAGE LOCKERS

Americans have too much stuff, and we have a hard time parting with it. There's a reason those hoarding television shows are so popular. Remember this: Buyers don't want to see your stuff, and they have a hard time looking past it. Clutter brings lower offers and makes your home more difficult to sell.

Having a big rental storage container parked on or near your driveway is better than leaving the stuff inside. Buyers know you're moving, so it's easier for them to see past those shipping units—they might be using one themselves! Still, nothing beats an off-site storage facility, which prevents any buyer from seeing your stuff at all.

Unless you are a minimalist, or you're able to be really harsh and honest with yourself, start packing up extraneous items as soon as possible and take them to a storage unit until you move.

CHAPTER 7

Getting Sale Ready, Part Three: Stage Your Home

When houses in your market are generally sitting unsold for a long time, you want to give yourself every advantage possible. Buyers have zero imagination when it comes to seeing a new house. They walk into a vacant home—or an occupied home with weird furniture or an unconventional layout—and they just freeze. Deer in headlights. Then they walk out and on to the next property.

Staging your home, vacant or occupied, means preparing it with the right colors, furniture, and style to attract the highest number of buyers. In fact, when buyers are more attracted to your home, they will stay inside longer, discovering all the things that made you buy it. Have you ever walked into a brand-new home being sold by the builder? The whole house looks amazing. Everything is color coordinated. There is just the right amount and right kind of art on the walls. The setup makes you want to live in that home. That's a staged house. No one lives there, but instead of showing a vacant home, builders have showroom-quality furnishings, and every space of the house has a purpose.

If you will be living in your home, you can still benefit from a home stager's services to help declutter and rid your space of old, worn, or outdated furniture or styles that could slow your selling process. A home stager will tour your house and make suggestions for placement of existing furnishings as well as suggestions for purchasing or renting additional items to give your home a more polished look and help it appeal to the broadest group of potential buyers. Staging is especially important for those odd spots in your home that don't have a clear purpose or maybe are intended for a function other than what you're using them for. For a vacant house, a home stager can provide an entire home's worth of furniture for a fee, but that can get pricey.

Want to save a few dollars? Here are DIY tips to help you the stage your house to sell fast.

KITCHEN

Grab a few nice-looking cookbooks and place them on the counter. If you don't have any already, a trip to the local thrift store will yield a ton of options, and you can even pick and choose some to match the color scheme of your kitchen. A small toaster or coffee pot, a container of utensils, and a bowl of fruit can really round out the kitchen. But be careful: You don't want the counters to look cluttered, especially if your kitchen is small or has little counter space.

Does your kitchen have anything notable like bookshelves for cookbooks or an outlet inside a cabinet to power the mixer? Does it have anything high-end like a wine refrigerator or a trash compactor? Hidden or unique features should have a card to draw attention to them. Make sure you highlight the extras that can set your home apart from the crowd.

Any extra storage space is a plus! If it isn't readily apparent from the outside, a well-placed note card will draw attention to the space.

DINING ROOM

Dining rooms are a formal place for most people, and yours should reflect that formal feeling. The dining room should have a table set with plates, silverware, glasses, and cloth napkins secured with a ring. If you don't have extra dishes lying about, you can find these items at a thrift store for almost nothing. Dust the table once a week so it stays fresh, and go the extra mile with a pretty centerpiece. A vase with live flowers looks beautiful for an open house. Just make sure to change out the arrangement or remove it altogether once the flowers start to wilt.

LIVING ROOM

The living room should be a comfortable space where people want to hang out. Show it off by using a nice, neutral-color couch. Throw in some decorative pillows for a splash of color or a bold print on an otherwise beige wall. Lamps can brighten up a dark space, and a mirror hung on a wall can make a small space look much larger.

A large flat-screen television is another trick I like to incorporate to make people *want* the house. The more luxurious looking your space is, the better, since most people are looking for something more—more square footage, more space, a better neighborhood. Show them this house is better than their current house, and make them want to own it. Check out thrift stores or local online communities for broken televisions if you don't have a flat screen already. It doesn't have to work to look good.

MASTER BEDROOM

The master bedroom should have a bed, a bedside table or nightstand, and a dresser. If you're not living in the home, use an air mattress or two to simulate a real bed and box spring set—it's one of the best staging tips I've ever heard. All you have to do is make sure it stays inflated! Make the bed as you normally would, and no one will ever know (unless they lie on it).

Be careful not to overstage. Don't make small bedrooms look smaller by using too large a bed or table. Don't make the bedside table look cluttered by placing too much stuff on it. A lamp, a clock, or a book will be enough to make the room look and feel like home.

ADDITIONAL BEDROOMS

Some people buying a house have children or are planning to have them soon. Show a bedroom as a gender-neutral baby's room with a crib, a few toys, and child-friendly pictures. Another bedroom could be made up for an older child or as an office space with a desk and a monitor or as a library with a bookcase and a reading chair. Just don't use clown wallpaper!

You want your house to appeal to the largest possible group of people, so give them ideas for how they can use other bedrooms if they don't yet have kids.

LAUNDRY ROOM

People go nuts for front-loader washing machines. Plus, a matching washer-and-dryer set gives a great finish to a room that most people might overlook. In the laundry room, throw a cute sign on the door, add detergent bottles free of drips or matching glass containers to hold the laundry soap and fabric softener, and use a tidy laundry basket to complete the look. These small touches will make your home stand out from the competition.

PRO·TIP *Think aspirational: Transform a house into a home people aspire to own. A staged home sells faster than an empty one.*

Buyers don't get the same feeling from an empty house as they do from one with furniture. Show them that your house will be a step up from their current home. Even though spending $1,000 to rent furniture may seem silly at first, you can make your home look put-together and modern, which means significantly higher offers. This makes that furniture totally worth the initial cost.

If you need more ideas or a visual aid, pick up a recent copy of a home magazine; you'll find plenty of staging examples. Pinterest is also an excellent source of design inspiration for every room in the house. Remember, you're trying to make the home look as appealing as possible to the largest possible group of people. As potential buyers walk through your home, you want them to be able to see themselves living there.

CHAPTER 8

Disclosure Statements

Houses are sold "as is" even when it is not specifically noted in the listing. Generally speaking, caveat emptor—Latin for "buyer, beware," meaning that the buyer alone is responsible for checking the quality of the home before purchasing—applies. However, most states have laws in place that require the seller to disclose any material defects to potential buyers. This means that if you know something is wrong with your house, you have to share that information with the people who are buying your home. In fact, most states don't let you off even that easily! They also include the phrase "or should know" in this disclosure requirement. If you know of or should know of a defect, you *must* disclose.

A material defect is something big—a shortcoming that can significantly affect the value of the home or poses an unusual risk. This is something that will most likely cost a lot of money to repair and is outside normal wear and tear. Issues like a cracked foundation or faulty electric wiring are examples of material defects. You must also disclose toxic or environmental issues such as persistent water in the basement, mold, and even problems outside your control, such as insect infestations.

These defects may be the sole reason you're selling. If that is the case, then you may be concerned that if you disclose these issues to buyers, they won't want to buy the house. However, this does not exempt you from disclosure. While it is true that homes in perfect condition sell faster and for more money, there truly is a buyer for every home, and sometimes patience pays off.

Your real estate agent should give you a seller's property disclosure (SPD) form to fill out. (If you are selling without an agent, you can find this form on your state's department of real estate website.) In my state of Colorado, the SPD is six pages long. Fill out this disclosure form carefully, completely, and honestly.

TRUE LIFE STORY

I once had to call an agent to get clarification after her seller checked "yes" in the box asking whether the house was an unremediated meth lab. I sure wasn't going to step foot into an unremediated meth house—let alone allow my clients to buy it! Luckily it was a mistake on the seller's form, and we still visited the house. Make sure to read any forms carefully!

If a problem has been repaired and is completely remedied, you do not have to disclose that issue. However, it is best practice to disclose both the issue and the date it was remedied so the buyers know you're being honest. Plus, neighbors talk. Chances are very high that if you had to deal with a massive issue, you complained to your neighbors about it, and chances are equally high that your former neighbors will talk to the new owners about it.

It is much better to be honest and risk losing a home sale than to come across as dishonest and open yourself up to potential lawsuits.

Change your thinking from "No one will buy it if they know about [insert issue here]" to "No one can sue me if I disclose that the house has [insert issue here]."

REAL LIFE DISCLOSURE STORIES
Idaho snake house
According to news reports, a couple in Idaho purchased a home in 2009 that turned out to have been built on a winter snake sanctuary, a place where snakes hibernate in the winter months. The buyers found multiple snakes in their home every day, and at times the water was undrinkable because of the snake's odor.

Before the couple purchased the home, they were informed of the snake infestation but signed a document at closing stating they were aware of the snakes. The home was priced so low, they felt it was a deal they could not pass up. Their real estate agent had assured them that it was a myth concocted by the previous owners to get out of paying their mortgage. The day the couple moved in, they saw eight snakes.

The document they had signed acknowledging the presence of snakes left them with no recourse—they were told about the issue and chose not to believe it. The previous homeowners and the bank that the new owners purchased it from had satisfied their notification requirements.

The couple eventually walked away from the home, ruining their credit and losing all the money they had in the home. They simply could not live there any longer.

This is just one example of why disclosure statements are extremely important.

Missouri spider house
Another environmental disclosure incident is known as the Spider House in St. Louis. In 2007, a couple purchased a home that they soon discovered was infested with brown recluse spiders—arachnids with a painful and, in some cases, deadly bite. The buyers found spiders everywhere in their home, from the pantry to the basement—even

in their shower. The couple sued both the former owners, who they claimed knew about the infestation but did not disclose it, and their insurance company, which refused to pay for damages. The insurance claimed that spiders were not covered in its policy. The policy excluded specifically insects, which spiders are technically not.

We're talking *infested*. During the trial, it was disclosed that the house had between 4,500 and 6,000 of these lethal spiders living in it, especially disturbing because the count took place in the winter, when spiders are least active and therefore least visible.

Both the sellers of the home and the buyers declared bankruptcy, with the buyers filing—and winning—a lawsuit against the sellers for nondisclosure. The insurance company for both parties happened to be the same company. The initial lawsuit against the insurance company ended in favor of the buyers, but the insurance company has yet to pay. Litigation is ongoing, the buyers have abandoned the home, and the situation is sure to be a mess for years to come.

Illinois water house

A friend's cousin decided a few years ago that she needed a change and no longer wanted to live in her house. She was just sick of it, so she put her house on the market and was surprised when it sold quickly for the full asking price. She needed to find a new house—and fast!

After searching for several weeks, she found what she thought was the house of her dreams, with a large yard, a fancy brick paver driveway, and a giant basement with high ceilings. And the basement was unfinished, so she could make it exactly how she wanted it. The house also came with four sump pumps and a very expensive generator hardwired to these sumps (foreshadowing!).

Just two weeks after she moved in, a rainstorm filled the basement with ten inches of standing water. She had brushed off her mother's questions about the giant sewer grate in the backyard, instead preferring to focus on the fact that it was a brand-new build.

Now she is embarking on a lawsuit against the builder for failure to disclose the very well-known water issues associated with the lot. She has successfully argued for a reduction in property value and subsequent reduction in property taxes, but this is going to cost her far more in lawsuits and ruined possessions. Not to mention the physical toll on her from the massive stress for years to come.

PRO·TIP *When in doubt, disclose. If you had a significant problem but have repaired it and it's no longer an issue, disclose it anyway. Also include how you fixed it, along with the name and contact information of any professional repair service used, any warranty information, and an approximate date of repair.*

Buyers will talk to their new neighbors, especially if there is an issue they're experiencing with their new home. Let's say you had a leak in your basement. If you're friendly with your neighbors, you'll ask them whether they are also having water in their basement. Regardless of their answer, you have now shared with the neighbors that you have water in your basement.

If you repair the issue, you may never get water in your basement again. Sharing with your buyers that you *used* to have water in the basement, but haven't since you made the repairs six years ago, will keep the buyers from being surprised when they have a conversation with their new neighbors—and keep them from wondering what else you didn't tell them.

Disclosure of past issues also helps protect you should an issue arise in the future. The buyers may contact you and ask you to cover the repairs, but you will be able to point out that you told them about the issue and they bought the home anyway.

Let's discuss the unpleasant topic of deaths in your home. Each state handles a death in a home in a different manner. Some states require disclosure no matter what the circumstances are, while other states require disclosure only if the death was sensational or infamous for some reason. For example, California requires disclosure if the death was a murder that happened in the past three years. Colorado regulation dictates that disclosing a death would unfairly stigmatize the property and therefore does not require disclosure. If you're aware of a death that happened in your home, be sure to understand the disclosure requirements before preparing to sell.

That said, you do not need to disclose every little thing that has ever been broken in the home, nor are you obligated to share issues outside the home that are readily apparent—such as close proximity to a cemetery or an airport. These items should be known to the buyer. One really common disclosure related to homes built before 1978, is the likely possibility that at least one layer of lead-based paint covers your walls. You are not responsible for removal of this paint, but your agent will need to provide a copy of the United States Environmental Protection Agency pamphlet "Protect Your Family from Lead in Your Home." The easiest way to do this is to upload it to the Multiple Listing Service, (MLS) as part of your disclosure documents.

Fill out the disclosure completely and honestly. Take a few days to really think about the home and any past issues you've had with it. Note any repairs that have 100 percent fixed the issue, and when in doubt, disclose the problem. Written disclosures significantly reduce lawsuits.

CHAPTER 9

Permits, Warranties, and More

When I bought my current home, it was a Fannie Mae foreclosure. This means the seller was the bank that had foreclosed on the property, and had no knowledge about anything in the home. It was not required to disclose anything either. Purchasing a foreclosure is truly a buyer-beware transaction.

I bought the home and did not check with the city to see whether the obvious addition in the back of the home had been permitted. I should have known better. When I say obvious addition, I mean that it was clear to anyone with eyeballs. The windows were drastically different from those in the rest of the house, the finish on the walls didn't match, and the wall separating the addition from the rest of the house was eight inches thick—obviously a former exterior wall. I could have gone to the permit office and checked into it, but I did not. I even purchased the home knowing I would be modifying it to the point of requiring permits, but I still did not go to the permit office.

A few months later, in the permit office, I presented my plans to the representatives, and they looked up my house in their database.

They said the addition I was planning to build was going up on top of nothing. They didn't have any record of the current addition to my house and couldn't approve the new one.

Of course, I freaked out. A city would be well within its rights to make you tear out the unpermitted work and rebuild—or worse, tear it out and not let you rebuild at all.

In my case, the unpermitted work violated the current setbacks (that is, the building restrictions imposed on property owners to measure distance from a property line where you can build). Luckily, our city was very generous. The building department worked with us to get approval for our existing project, then approved an amended version of our new project to include the existing space. This space violated the setback laws but was grandfathered in because it was already standing. The new space that we were going to build, however, had to conform to the setbacks.

Have you had any work done on your property? Did you pull the proper permits and have the work inspected and approved by the building inspector? Did you pass all your inspections and get a final certificate of occupancy? A certificate of occupancy (also called occupancy permit) comes from the building inspector and certifies that the property is ready to be lived in, that it meets current building codes, and has passed all the inspections. If you have followed the proper procedure, prepare a binder or a folder with all of this documentation to pass along to the new owner of your home. Doing this shows that you followed all the proper procedures and also gives your buyers peace of mind that the rest of the home has been well taken care of too.

If you haven't pulled permits—and you should have—now is the time to rectify this situation. Simple fixes like changing a door handle or swapping out a light fixture need not be recorded, but contact your local building department to see what your options are when trying to permit projects long after the fact. Be prepared to pay a fine for not obtaining a permit at the time the work was performed, and be prepared to wait for the papers to process. The inspection process to permit work that is already in existence can be lengthy and varies by city. Start this by contacting the permit office in your county to verify whether a permit is required for the work that was completed.

HOME WARRANTY

A home warranty is an insurance policy that protects you against certain system failures. For instance, if the furnace goes out during the warranty's time frame—typically one year—the home warranty will cover the cost of the repair.

In a seller's market, offering a home warranty is not necessary. Buyers are lining up to purchase your home, and there is no need to spend the extra money.

But what if you find yourself trying to sell in a buyer's market? You need to do everything you can to make your home stand out among all the other properties so that buyers choose yours.

Offering a home warranty might seem like a great idea, but what are you really giving prospective buyers? I'm not a fan of a home warranty. I've purchased a few houses that came with one and felt as if the sellers had wasted their money. I don't use home warranties, even when they are "paid for" by the seller. Why? Because the seller hasn't really paid for much of anything!

A home warranty sounds great in theory, but the reality is much different. A home warranty covers a variety of appliances and systems in the house, and the specifics will be listed in the policy. However, to have those appliances serviced by the home warranty company, you must pay a service-call fee, which is around $80. This is just to get the repair person out to look at the appliance or system and diagnose the problem.

Home warranties are not worth the paper they are printed on. It seems that whatever is wrong with an item is not covered under the warranty, or if the malfunction is, then the warranty covers only up to a certain dollar amount, and you are on the hook for the rest. You also have to use only the contractors the home warranty company specifies, and there is generally no negotiation or shopping around for a better price.

I would not recommend offering a home warranty unless the buyers ask for it. In fact, I wouldn't even mention it. However, if you're in a buyer's market, and they do ask, it may be worth offering one to get your home sold, especially if your competition is offering one too.

TAXPAYER RELIEF ACT

The IRS generally does not give—it taketh away. Prior to 1997, home sellers wishing to defer capital gains taxes were required to purchase a new home that was more expensive than the one they were selling within a certain time frame. Those rules are gone now, and in 1997, the IRS gave home sellers a very generous gift with the American Taxpayer Relief Act.

Section 121, also referred to as the two-out-of-five rule, is a federal law that allows you to avoid paying capital gains taxes on the appreciation of your primary residence. This law exempts up to $250,000 if you're single and up to $500,000 if you're married, provided you live in the home as your personal residence *and* have owned it for two of the past five years.

Note that I said *appreciation* of your primary residence. Appreciation is the difference between what you paid for it—including any improvements, repairs, rehabs, and upgrades—and what you are selling it for now.

For the sake of clarity, you subtract the amount of money you've spent on the home (purchase price plus any improvements, repairs, or upgrades) from the total sales price to determine the amount of appreciation. You are looking to avoid capital gains taxes, so you want your appreciation to be as low as you can make it. You should be able to back up these costs with receipts from contractors and supply stores in case you are audited.

Let's do some quick math. You paid $100,000 for the house back in 1987. You're selling it now, and it has been your primary residence since you bought it. Your selling price is $550,000, and you put $50,000 into a brand-new kitchen four years ago.

Your appreciation is $550,000 minus $50,000 minus $100,000, for a total of $400,000. Since you and your spouse have lived in the home together all these years, you qualify for the up-to-$500,000 exemption, so every penny of that $400,000 appreciation is yours to keep, free and clear with no taxes owed.

Like any other government program, there are a few rules you must follow, of course. You can claim this exemption only once every two years. The property must be your primary residence, and that "living/owning for two years" stipulation is set in stone. Even one day early will leave you with paying capital gains taxes of 15–20 percent, depending on your tax bracket. While you can certainly list your home, accept an offer, go through all the contingencies, and get all the way to closing before the two years are up, you cannot sign the documents or transfer ownership until two years have passed to take advantage of this offer.

Even with the accompanying rules, it's a pretty sweet deal, and you don't get sweet deals from the IRS every day. If you have any questions about whether you qualify for this fantastic gift, ask your tax professional before you list your home.

CHAPTER 10

Your Next Home

Generally speaking, you shouldn't start looking for your next home until you can afford the down payment. If you have a home to sell, you may have equity that you will be using to make the down payment on your new house. To access that equity, you will need to sell your current home.

This scenario is a catch-22. You can't buy until you sell, and you can't sell until you have a place to buy.

In a balanced market, this isn't a difficult endeavor. There are enough homes on the market that you can generally find one you like after you have an accepted offer on your current home.

In a buyer's market, accepting an offer on your current home before finding a new one to buy is more financially advantageous. Otherwise, you run the risk of needing to cancel your contract when you can't sell your home, losing your earnest money if you do not cancel your contract in time, paying two mortgages until you can sell your home, and even risking financial ruin if you cannot afford both homes.

Conversely, in a seller's market, homes go quickly, and unless you have a unique house that will appeal to very few buyers, it will be easy to sell and far more difficult to find a home to move in to once you've sold. In a seller's market, many times you will see post-closing occupancy agreements, in which the sellers essentially rent their old home back from the buyer while they continue to look for a new place to buy.

CAN YOU AFFORD TWO MORTGAGES?

Ultimately, your move comes down to what you're most comfortable with. Do you have a hefty bank account that will let you carry two mortgages without breaking you? How long can you pay both mortgages easily? Is renting the property an option? Can your finances withstand a significant price reduction should the home fail to sell even after you have moved out?

TRUE LIFE STORY

My friends Ron and Linda owned a nice home in a large city. Ron decided to change jobs and found a new position in a town about thirty miles north. Not an insurmountable drive, but he preferred a shorter commute. He and Linda had two small children, and an hour in the car each way would have had him leaving just as they woke up and arriving home just as they were going to bed.

They put their home on the market, received an offer and accepted it, and started their home search in the new town. They found the perfect house and started packing up their things. They had ample savings and purchased their new home before closing on the old one so they could have time to move out without feeling rushed.

A few days before closing, their real estate agent called to inform them that the buyer's financing had fallen through. This was in 2008, when the housing market had completely dropped through the floor. There were no buyers for their old home, and they had already purchased their new one. They decided to rent the home for a year and see whether the market would improve a little later. They chose a tenant who looked great on paper. High credit score, no outstanding debts, great-paying job as an attorney. And not just any attorney—he was a highly paid litigator.

Almost as soon as he moved in, the problems started. He would request repairs at any time of day or night. He would threaten legal action for the most trivial of instances, yet he paid his rent on time every month.

You see, if he had not paid on time, Ron and Linda could have started the eviction process. Our state is very landlord friendly, and the tenant would have been removed from the home easily for nonpayment of rent.

But he was obnoxiously demanding, knowing that Ron and Linda would be forced to acquiesce as long as he continued to pay the rent on time every month. Even worse, Ron and Linda encountered just as soft a market in 2009, when his lease was up for renewal. This made them feel obligated to renew his lease, fearing that they wouldn't find another tenant.

He ended up purchasing the home from them when his lease was up in 2010, using his intimate knowledge of the property to negotiate the purchase price down with a thoroughly defeated Ron and Linda, who were ready to be rid of both the house and him.

They lost a lot of money when they sold the home and could have avoided the entire experience if they had waited to close on the new home until after they had sold the old one.

WHERE ARE YOU MOVING?

If your reason for selling is want versus need, or if you can't afford two mortgages—and do not wish to become a landlord if your sale falls through—I would strongly recommend having your home under contract before starting your new search. Further, you should close on the old home before purchasing the new one. Even at the last minute, contracts can fall through. If you can't swing two payments, and you are in a buyer's market, purchasing the new home first is a bad idea.

If you are moving out of the area completely, consider renting in the new location for a short time to allow your old home to sell and also to give yourself time to learn the new area.

WHAT IF YOU CANNOT SELL?

In a seller's market, almost every home will sell. If you have an odd house, it's going to take longer, but eventually you will find a buyer. In a buyer's market, selling your home takes much longer, unless it's absolutely perfect, and even then, a quick sale is rare.

What happens if selling your home takes longer than you had anticipated? Go back to your why: Why are you selling your home?

If you are selling because you want to, you can simply take your house off the market and try again at a more favorable time. You can also lower the price until the home sells or offer creative financing to the buyers, like holding the mortgage yourself—either in part or in full. Another option is to rent out your house and try again later. However, being a landlord should not be a choice you take lightly. If a rental is managed carelessly, it can cost you thousands of dollars in missed rent, damages, and eviction charges, not to mention the toll that the added stress will take on you.

If you are selling because of a move or otherwise similar need to sell, reducing the price is the fastest way to a sale.

In every market, there are people who are looking for a deal. There are people who can't really afford the area but want to live there anyway, and there are people who will buy based solely on price. In a hot seller's market, reducing the price isn't going to be as necessary as it is in a colder market, but either way, a lower price leads to a faster sale.

WHAT IF YOU CAN'T FIND ANYTHING TO BUY?

Selling in a hot market is awesome! The house sells fast, and you most likely have a lot of interest regardless of the condition. But while being a *seller* in a seller's market is awesome, being a *buyer* in a seller's market is not so great. Once your home is sold, what do you do if you can't find a house to buy?

In this scenario, renting is the best option, but when renting short-term, you can expect to pay a higher monthly rent. You don't want to sign a lease for three to six months, find the next property a couple of weeks later, and then be stuck with the rental for extra months you don't need it for. With this in mind, maybe it'd be better to find an alternative.

You can ask for the buyers of your property to rent it back to you until you find your new property. This is common in hot seller's markets and offers the most flexibility. You sign a post-closing occupancy agreement, which is similar to a lease, and pay them rent either monthly or all up front.

Buying and selling in a seller's market is truly a balancing act. Just remember: You have the most power *before* you sign the purchase contract from your buyer.

TRUE LIFE STORY

Ron and Linda's bad housing luck didn't stop at the eventual sale of their old, big-city home. They lived in their new, perfect home for about eight years. Ron moved up in his company at the same time their neighborhood started to turn in a direction they did not like, so they decided to put their home on the market. The city was experiencing a very hot seller's market, and their desirable home sold for above asking price on the same day it was listed. Great, right?

Not so fast. Linda is a woman with discriminating taste, and not just any home will do for her. She wanted to be in a covenant-controlled neighborhood, which means a home-owners' association is in place to regulate what you can or cannot do with your home and property. One of Linda's biggest reasons for moving was that a new neighbor did not keep his yard looking nice and had no respect for his fellow neighbors. She also wanted to live in a nice neighborhood and found a great house—until the home inspection turned up too many deal breakers for her.

The next home they put under contract seemed perfect, until the inspection revealed no issues with the home but issues with the next-door neighbors—specifically their dogs.

They barked. All the time. During the three-hour home inspection, the dogs were in the backyard barking as loud as they could, nonstop.

Linda and her husband ended up putting seven different properties under contract, only to have six of them fall through for one reason or another. While they were renting their old home back from the buyers, they had a timeline, and they could not continue indefinitely.

Feeling the pressure to find a home, they finally settled for a property that was smaller than their old house, with a tinier yard and less room.

Recognize your needs and particularity. Be honest with yourself. If you know that finding a new property is going to take you a long time, start your search even before you list your house. If you know you're easy to please, you may wish to postpone the house hunting until after you have a contract on your own house.

CHAPTER 11
Fair Housing Laws

You don't know what you don't know, yet ignorance is not a valid reason to break the law. You cannot discriminate against prospective buyers based on a variety of factors, including race, sex, and religion.

In fact, so many people practiced discrimination that Title VIII of the Civil Rights Act of 1968, commonly called the Fair Housing Act, prohibits sellers and landlords from discriminating against a buyer or renter based on:

- Race or color
- Religion
- Sex
- National origin
- Familial status
- Disability

HOW TO AVOID VIOLATING THE FAIR HOUSING ACT

You should not be present during the showing of your home. It makes buyers uncomfortable, and when they're uncomfortable, they won't want to buy your home.

If you're not at the home, you won't see them. You won't know whether they have children, what their race is, whether they have any disabilities—you won't know anything about them if they choose to make an offer.

Don't ask.

The less you know about your buyer, the better off you are and the more objective you will be. None of this matters when someone is buying your home. You aren't going to be living there anymore, so someone who has kids is not your problem. Someone who practices a different religion is not your problem. A buyer who is of a different nationality, color, or race is not your concern. It does not matter.

Do they have the funds to close, and can they do so in a time frame that suits you? Those are the only things you should consider when accepting an offer. Do not open yourself up to potential lawsuits because of issues that do not matter. Ask your agent for guidance about Fair Housing laws.

PRO·TIP *When it comes to selling your house, the only thing that matters is whether the buyers can uphold their end of the bargain. All they need to do is close on the house.*

CHAPTER 12

Interviewing Real Estate Agents

Not all real estate agents are the same. Actually, strike that. Many of them are the same. They're just not very good at being an agent. There is no shortage of agents who do not know their market, cannot accurately gauge prices, and have no clue what they're doing in general.

There is an extremely low barrier to entry as an agent. You take a course, pass an exam, complete a background check, and *poof*, you are now a licensed agent. No knowledge of real estate or the local market, no sales experience, and no negotiation skills are required to become licensed. The course doesn't teach you much about real estate in general and nothing at all about how to sell. The course teaches how to pass the real estate licensing exam and nothing more.

When I first received my license and started working for a very seasoned agent, she said, "Congratulations on passing your test. Now let's get to work on teaching you everything you didn't learn in class—which is everything." We had a good laugh, but I soon realized she was absolutely right. Nothing I had learned during the licensing coursework had prepared me to help people buy or sell their home. Nothing.

I had been buying and selling real estate as an investor for almost twenty years. I was fairly sure I knew what I was doing—certainly I had a leg up on others who had just graduated but did not have my level of experience, right? Nope. Not even close. The behind-the-scenes part of being an agent is far different from the side the public sees. If I was starting at square one, how helpful could other agents be—people with no investing background—straight out of school?

In a hot market, real estate agents come out of the woodwork, with everyone under the mistaken impression that selling real estate is easy, lucrative, and fun. Formerly licensed agents change their status back to active, bored housewives feel it's a surefire way to riches, and people unhappy with their current career path decide now is the time to make the switch.

In a hot market, selling real estate *is* easy. Houses sell themselves: Buyers scramble to purchase any house for which the sellers will accept their offer, ask very little from the seller, and in general make it very easy for the sale to go through. Everyone is on his or her best behavior, and the agent simply has to make sure the timeline is followed, an easy task in today's electronic age. Spend a few minutes punching everything into your phone's calendar, and set reminders.

In a hot, hot market, selling real estate *is* lucrative. Commissions for buying or selling homes hover around 3 percent per side. For example, a sales price of $200,000 would earn $6,000 in commissions.

- According to Payscale.com, the average real estate agent's salary is $45,810.
- According to Realtor.com, the average home sales price in 2016 was $412,222.94.

Dividing the average sales price by the average salary gets you roughly nine houses per agent per year. I wouldn't call $45,000 lucrative. It's not chump change, but it's not going to make you rich.

I *do* think selling real estate is fun. I love looking at houses, figuring out how to rehab the ugly ones, and admiring the finishes on the nice ones. Unless the home is horribly odorous—think multiple cats with an unchanged litter box—I can happily spend an hour in a home just looking around. I love looking at layouts, unique features, and interesting color combinations. I've rehabbed enough houses to give great suggestions on how to upgrade a home from its current state to *wow*. But that doesn't make me a good agent.

To be a good agent, I must know my market, accurately estimate housing prices, know my market, be available to my clients when they need me, and know my market. (See a trend?) What the general public does not realize about agents, is that there are a lot of buyers who start the buying process and then stop, which is frustrating for everyone. Agents spend a lot of money and time on advertising and attracting clients, which goes to waste when people don't actually purchase homes.

PRO·TIP *Not every agent is the same, and to have a great selling experience, you'll need to do a little homework. Don't just hire anyone from a sign.*

My sister hired someone from a sign and had a selling experience fraught with anger, frustration, and confusion throughout the entire process. Her agent did not work well with first timers. She routinely did not give proper advice, glossed over things she felt weren't important, and did nothing when the eventual buyers missed closing date after closing date. She gave no notice to my sister that the date had changed and no information about why. She just went radio silent.

My sister also used her to purchase her next property, and the agent was equally unhelpful on the buying side too. I sat on the sidelines, hearing bits from my sister, who clearly didn't understand what was going on. If this is your first time selling, make sure your agent knows this and works well with first timers.

Despite this horror story, you actually *should* pay attention to the names on the signs in your neighborhood. In my own neighborhood, there are two women who list about 85 percent of the properties. While you shouldn't pick someone *just* from their sign, you should take note if you're seeing the same name over and over. The name or names you repeatedly see should be near the top of your list of agents to interview.

While they aren't going to be the least expensive listing agents, they have name recognition and most likely a great website where buyers go to look for properties.

Here are some things to consider and questions to ask before deciding on an agent to list and sell your house.

QUESTIONS TO ASK AN AGENT

How many homes have you sold this year?

Not having sold many homes in the past shouldn't be an automatic disqualification—everybody starts off at the beginning. But if you need to sell your home quickly and are up against a slower market, perhaps using a new agent isn't the better choice for you.

Experienced agents have a vast network they can rely on to help get your home sold. They have past clients who hopefully are happy with their purchase and who have friends who might be looking for a home. They have a large mailing list to advertise your listing with and more name recognition within the local area. Name recognition goes far in real estate, and seeing the same name on signs all around the city can give a sense of trust that the home is what it appears to be.

However, if your market isn't slow or you aren't in a rush to sell, using an agent who hasn't sold a house before can actually get you more attention and possibly sell your house faster. A newer agent will have fewer clients and will be able to give you more personal attention than an established agent who is part of a large team.

At what price would you list my house, and why?

This is a very important question to ask potential agents. Listen to their reasons, not just the dollar amount. An agent who can back up his or her price recommendation with facts, such as lists of similar properties that have recently sold near you—called comparable properties, or comps—has a far better chance of selling your home at or near the recommended price than someone who pulls a number out of thin air.

While it is tempting to go with the agent who gives you the highest list price, that doesn't mean your house will sell for that price.

One of the worst things you can do when listing your home is to overprice it.

You see, houses don't necessarily sell at their asking price. They sell for what they are worth. Asking $500,000 for a house that's worth only $475,000 may not seem like a big deal, but that extra $25,000 can cause your home to sit on the market, the listing growing stale, while other, more appropriately priced houses are selling.

You may be thinking, "Well, buyers can just give me a lower offer."

This thought process may seem like a good approach. After all, you can't list for $450,000, get a full-price offer, and then ask the buyers to pay more. But listing high with the expectation of a slightly lower offer does not help you get more money for your house. As homes gather market time—called days on market, or DOM—a perception that something is wrong with the house grows, especially in a hot market, in which every other house is selling quickly.

The questions "At what price would you list my house, and why?" are particularly important in weeding out agents who don't have your best interests in mind. Don't let a flashy list price land you an agent that doesn't know his or her market.

Listings are the bread and butter of real estate agent income. Once your home is listed with a specific agent, it's easier to just lower the price when the house isn't selling than to cancel the contract, find a new agent, and relist.

Also, beware of the bait-and-switch agent who suggests a high list price but is not able to back it up with facts. Do not fall for this trick and potentially cost yourself a quick sale because of an overpriced house.

How do you market a home?
A house will sell because of its price, location, amenities, and accessibility. Accessibility means a couple of different things: both the access to the house, meaning you allow showings with little or no advance notice, as well as the accessibility of information about the house to prospective buyers.

It's extremely important to know how the agent will market your house. You want to be sure he or she is putting the property on the MLS. Any agent who does not should be automatically disqualified. The MLS is the number one way agents get up-to-the-minute information about properties for sale.

In addition to listing your home on the MLS, your agent should also blast it out to all the other real estate sites—like Zillow, Trulia, Redfin, and so on. The MLS includes agent-only access, but those other sites are public, and many buyers start their home search on one of these sites.

Other marketing ideas include open houses, postcard campaigns to the agent's mailing list, 360-degree photography tours or a video walkthrough, a broker's open house, and a shared preview of the listing with the agent's office and clients. Newspaper listings are no longer as important or relevant as they once were. While it certainly cannot hurt to have your home listed in the newspaper, this should not be the center of a marketing campaign.

The object of this exercise is to sell the home, so you want it listed everywhere it can be and marketed in as many different ways as possible. You never know where buyers are coming from or where they are looking.

What is your favorite method of communication?

This question is very important, although at first glance, it may seem frivolous. You are the boss in this relationship! It's *your* house and *your* money. You should be able to communicate the way you are most comfortable. If you have a job outside your home, do you think your boss wants you to receive phone calls from your agent every two hours? Probably not. If your agent is not very tech savvy, but you prefer to text or e-mail your communications, you want to know that before you hire him or her. On the other hand, if you want phone calls, and your agent will only text you, you want to know that too.

It is very important to choose an agent whose communication style matches yours so you get timely information about any offers, questions from potential buyers, and any other communication necessary to get your home sold.

Do you have references from recent sellers?

An agent who hasn't yet sold a home won't have any references, but that's not necessarily a red flag. But an agent who has been doing this for a while and has no references? I'd pass. Over the span of an entire career, every agent will come across at least one client who cannot be pleased. There will be things outside the agent's control that could change the entire transaction, and there isn't an agent on the planet who has a 100 percent success rate long term.

When you're following up with the references, make sure to ask what they liked about the agent, how responsive the agent was, what hiccups they experienced through the transaction, how long it took to sell their house, how close to the suggested list price the home actually sold for, and whether they would work with the agent again. You would be surprised at who is included on reference lists.

PRO·TIP *Don't just ask for recommendations. Agents likely aren't going to give you the names of clients with whom they've had a bad experience. Instead, ask for the past five clients.*

On average, what percentage of the original list price do your properties sell for?

Anyone can list homes for sale at very high prices. Remember the bait-and-switch agent from before? A bait-and-switch agent does not help get your home sold faster when he or she lists it high and then drops the price. In fact, quite the opposite. Listed too high, your home will languish on the market, while more reasonably priced properties will sell to buyers that could have been yours!

Your agent should be selling homes very near their list price; this says the agent knows the local market and is familiar with its current state.

An agent who routinely lists high and then sells at significantly lower prices should not be your agent. Unless there had been a significant and swift downturn in your local market, this should be a big red flag. Ask your agent to provide you with a list of all homes he or she has listed in the past six to twelve months, both listing and sales prices along with the DOM.

I want to keep up with the competition. Will you show me competing homes?

Your agent should recommend a fairly tight price range in which you should list your home and have comps to back up his or her suggestion. While you are preparing to list your home, ask your agent to set you up with a search for homes similar to yours in price, features, and area. You'll want to keep an eye on the competition.

By watching how similar homes are priced, you can get a feel for where you should list your home too. While your agent should recommend a price range, ultimately where you list is your choice. Listing at the top of the range isn't always in your best interest. Selling fast could be more important than selling for top dollar in your case.

If you're having trouble deciding on a listing price or if you disagree with your agent's recommendation, ask him or her to show you a few of the competing listings—both at the price you want and the price the agent suggests. Ultimately, the market will dictate what your home sells for, and sometimes seeing where other properties are listed can help you settle on a price.

If I hire you and this does not work out, how do I cancel my contract?

Despite your best efforts, you may end up choosing an agent you ultimately feel you can no longer work with. You should know up front how you can end the contract. Do you just cancel the agreement? Do you need to go through the agent's broker?

This is where problems can arise with your listing contract. Your contract is actually not with the agent but rather with his or her employing broker (unless the agent is the employing broker). If you are unhappy with the service you are getting from the agent, consider speaking with the employing broker to request a different agent. The broker can direct you to someone in the office who will be better able to help you. Let the employing broker know the exact issue so he or she can match you up with an agent who is more suitable. Brokers will want to do everything in their power to keep you as a client.

While you may feel awkward requesting someone else, do it anyway. Most agents do not want to hold clients to a contract they are not happy with, and if you're not feeling happy with your agent, chances are he or she already knows it. This is probably your largest sale to date, and you should be comfortable with the agent you have hired to represent you and your interests.

You will most likely need to sign a dissolution of agency agreement, whereby you are both released of the obligations of the contract. The agent will provide you with a list of any and all buyers who have viewed the home during the time it was under contract with him or her. This list is typically good for one year, which means that if anyone on the list ends up purchasing the property within that time frame, the agent is owed a commission. This is standard procedure and should not cause you any alarm.

What commission do you charge?

This is the part that no one likes to talk about. A real estate agent's time and knowledge is worth money. You don't work for free, and you cannot expect your agent to work for free either.

At first glance, it can seem like the listing agent is charging a lot of money for very little work. The agent lists your house on the MLS and then sits back and waits for the offers to pour in. Before I was licensed, this was exactly my thought too.

But then I listed my first house.

Coordinating showings isn't difficult, but it does take time. There are many phone calls from other agents asking all sorts of questions about the house, the neighborhood, the sellers, their motivation for moving, and so on.

After the home receives offers, the agent must read through the entire document to decipher what is being offered and what is being requested. The devil is in the details, and some offers come with a very high initial price that is quickly wiped away by concession requests that another, slightly lower offer many not have.

After an offer is accepted, there are timelines to keep and deadlines to meet. Further negotiations can always pop up after inspection and appraisal.

The adage is true: You get what you pay for. An agent who offers a significant discount on commission may deliver only the bare minimum when it comes to service and support. If this is your first sale, commission shouldn't be your only consideration. Commission rates are absolutely negotiable, but as the seller you should expect to pay around 3 percent to your listing agent and another 3 percent to the buyer's agent. If a discounted rate is offered, ask exactly what that covers and how it's divvied up between the agents before you sign a contract.

The seller should always offer the buyer's agent their full commission. The buyer's agent does even more work than the seller's agent does and they have earned that commission. On top of that, they are choosing the order in which they show homes to their clients. While it is technically illegal to allow bias to conflict with client interest, the buyer's agents can choose to show those homes with a lower offered commission last so that the buyers are more likely to find a home in the higher-commission listings they're shown first.

Also ask your agent for an estimate of fees, including anything outside the commission. Many agents wrap all fees into the commission, but others will have additional charges such as document storage fees. You do not want any surprises about fees, and this is a question that agents get asked frequently. Know everything before you sign a contract, or you may find yourself on the hook for a lot more than you thought.

TRUE LIFE STORY

I once received a phone call the night before closing from the agent who was representing me as a buyer, telling me about an additional $200 fee she had forgotten to share with me beforehand. I felt put on the spot and agreed to pay it. But I also felt misled, and I never used her again. I would have been far more willing to pay this fee if it had been disclosed up front.

ASK QUESTIONS

If you don't know something, ask. Don't pretend to understand something or assume it's not a big deal. If you're confused, ask questions until you are no longer confused. There's no such thing as a stupid question.

It is far better to ask as many questions as necessary, than to get hit with a big fee because you didn't ask enough questions. If your agent makes you feel stupid, they aren't the right agent for you. This is a big sale—most likely the biggest of your life, so it does not matter what your agent thinks of you, it only matters how the deal ends.

Your agent has most likely sold homes many times before. Sometimes an agent may have done something so many times, he or she forgot to teach you the basics. Your agent isn't willfully misleading you and isn't trying to hide anything from you. If you have a question, ask it. Your agent should want to help you out. And if yours doesn't, then get a new one.

CHECKLIST: QUESTIONS TO ASK YOUR AGENT
- [ ] How many homes have you sold this year?
- [ ] At what price would you list my home, and why?
- [ ] How do you market a home?
- [ ] What is your favorite method of communication?
- [ ] Can I ask for references from your last five clients?
- [ ] On average, what percentage of the original list price do your properties sell for?
- [ ] I want to keep up with the competition. Will you show me competing homes?

☐ If I hire you and this does not work out, how do I cancel my contract with you?

☐ What commission do you charge?

LOCAL MLS ACCESS

We touched on this earlier, but let's cover it again because it's important. If an agent has no MLS access, he or she is not the agent for you.

There isn't just one MLS, either. In fact, just a few years ago, there were more than 1,400 separate MLS systems. Consolidation has brought that number down considerably, but it's still really, really high.

I live in northern Colorado. My local area has three MLS systems. They all used to share information, but they had a spat and are currently not speaking to one another. Which means that if I need good information about an area, I can search records only for the MLS system that I belong to. This is not a big deal for me because I specialize in one city, and every listing in that city goes onto the MLS of which I am a member.

A fellow agent and friend of mine isn't as lucky. He covers an area south of me that has traditionally been covered by both listing systems. He now has to subscribe to both to best serve his clients. If he didn't, he wouldn't be able to serve half of his clients or cover half his area.

Make sure the agent you hire has access not only to the MLS but also to the MLS that services your city specifically. If your city happens to have more than one system, your agent should have access to both.

REALTOR VERSUS REAL ESTATE AGENT

In recent years, the National Association of Realtors created an initiative to differentiate a Realtor from someone who simply has a real estate license. All Realtors have a real estate license, but not all people with a real estate license are Realtors.

A Realtor is a member of the National Association of Realtors (NAR). NAR requires its members to uphold a code of ethics by which other agents are not bound. However, this doesn't mean that agents who are not Realtors have no ethics.

The code of ethics is not that much different from the duties a real estate agent is bound to uphold by state licensing boards. Fiduciary responsibility is the top duty an agent is required to follow—meaning he or she is required to put your needs first regardless of whether he or she is an agent or a Realtor.

EXPERIENCED AGENT VERSUS EAGER NEWBIE

An experienced agent is going to be able to walk you through the transaction smoothly. Experienced agents have already been through almost anything that might pop up during your transaction, and if they haven't, chances are high they know someone who has. But experience comes with a price: time. Your experienced agent has such a volume of clients, he or she most likely needs a team of people to help out. This means you'll get very little face time with the actual agent, and a member of his or her team will be assigned to you instead. This is not a huge deal if you're prepared for it, but if you're basing your decision on access to the agent, make sure you voice that ahead of time.

With that experience and client load comes an almost guarantee that this is an agent's only job. This means that your agent—or one of his or her representatives—will be able to answer questions and be available to you during the entire process.

An eager newbie may need supplemental income from another job until his or her real estate career takes off, which means that agent may not be able to receive phone calls during the business day. If you have a question, it might have to wait. If another agent or that agent's buyer has a question about your property, that's going to have to wait too. A buyer may not want to wait and might simply move on to the next house on the list.

On the other hand, the eager newbie probably doesn't have many or even any other clients—and may have a spouse who can provide financial support as he or she tries to make a go of it, which means you get undivided attention.

Every agent was new at one time, and every agent had a first client. If your need to sell is not urgent, your market is balanced or even a seller's market, and you have a recommendation for someone who is new to the scene, feel free to give the agent a chance. But if your urgency is high, an experienced agent could be a better fit for your needs.

BE ON THE SAME PAGE AS YOUR AGENT

Your agent is your firewall and will receive far more phone calls than he or she will share with you because many of them involve questions your agent knows the answers to. Other agents call your agent rather than you to ask things like "When is the ideal closing time?" and "What is the lowest price the sellers will accept?" Without fail, every time I list a home, I get this question. I hate this question for a lot of reasons, but mostly because as the seller's agent, I'm the one who is expected to show my hand, while the buyer's agent gives up nothing.

PRO·TIP *As the selling agent, when I receive questions about the price, I always respond, "We will consider all written offers." I encourage you to instruct your agent to say something similar. In real estate, a verbal offer is not binding. There isn't anything to discuss until you receive an offer in writing.*

Buyers truly interested in the house will be interested enough to write an offer. If they aren't interested enough to write up an offer, you don't want to waste your time with them anyway.

TRUE LIFE STORY

I was representing a buyer who drove past a newly listed home in her desired neighborhood on the way to a friend's house. She called me and asked if I would contact the seller's agent to discuss an offer with a home sale contingency, which means the purchase was dependent on the sale of the buyer's home.

My client had a lovely home to sell in a very popular neighborhood during the hottest seller's market our town had ever seen. Her home had many features that would produce a bidding war once the house was on the market, but she didn't want to get stuck with two mortgages as she had in a previous, cooler market when her existing home sale had fallen through.

I explained the circumstances to the seller's agent, who seemed offended that I would even call her on the phone to discuss such an offer, let alone suggest that her client accept such an offer. She told me point-blank to have my client first list and sell her home and then write the offer on the house she wanted to purchase, if it was still available.

Fast-forward two months, and my client had found another home while this house was still sitting unsold. The seller's friend informed the seller that my client had expressed interest in writing an offer, but the seller's agent said she wasn't interested in offers with contingencies.

I had never written the offer. Both the buyer and I were convinced the seller would not accept any contingent offer based on the conversation I'd had with the listing agent.

That seller was absolutely livid with her agent when she found out. Of course, no one knows if she would have actually accepted an offer with that contingency. I'm sure her agent felt she was acting in the best interests of the client, given how fast homes were selling at that time. Her agent was wrong.

Make sure you share with your agent what sort of offer and contingencies you will consider and which you will not consider. I recommend reviewing every offer that comes in, including those with contingencies. However, if you know that you absolutely will not consider a certain contingency, share that with your agent. There is no need to waste anyone's time.

Price is also a key factor for you and your agent to understand. While again I recommend allowing any offer to be written, as a seller, I'm not a fan of lowball offers. The comment "We will consider all reasonable offers" is enough to deter most bargain hunters yet conveys your willingness to negotiate.

As the owner of the property, *you* are the boss of the sale. If you truly believe the home is worth what you're asking, you can instruct your agent to dismiss any offer less than your desired amount.

I did this for one house I was selling before I was licensed. I knew my home was worth a certain amount, but the market was a little soft. After receiving some ridiculously low offers, 25 percent below asking price in one instance, I simply told my agent not to present any offers below a certain price and to share that with the agent making the offer.

PRO·TIP *Your agent is required by law to present any offer unless otherwise instructed by you.*

CHAPTER 13

Contracts and Offers

Once you have committed to an agent, he or she will most likely ask you to put that in writing by signing an exclusive listing agreement, which means that that agent is the only one with whom you are legally listing your home.

EXCLUSIVE LISTING CONTRACTS

Read this exclusive listing contract carefully, as you are legally bound to it regardless of whether or not you understand it. This contract will have both your name and the listing agent's name, the employing broker under whom the listing agent works, and your property's address. In general, the exclusive listing agreement states that should the property sell, or if the agent procures a ready, willing, and able buyer, the listing agent is due a commission.

The language in this agreement is extremely important because a sale is not the only way the agent earns commission. If he or she finds a buyer—but you ultimately decide you are not going to sell the house—you could be on the hook for the full commission. Before you sign this contract, ask the agent how you can cancel it, should you change your mind. Houses get pulled from the market all the time: Maybe you lose your job, adult children decide to move back in with you, or you just decide you can't move away from the house you've lived in your entire life. Whatever the reason, make sure you know how to get out of a contract *before* you sign it.

Another reason to cancel the contract? Your agent doesn't perform. All agents are not created equal, and some will sing a good song just to get the contract but will not actually follow through with their promises once they've got the property listing.

PRO·TIP *As with anything else in this process, ask questions— and keep asking for clarification—until you under- stand.*

While you will most likely be signing an exclusive listing agreement, there are other contracts available. An open listing means that any agent can promote and sell the property. While this sounds good on paper, the reality is that you could end up having *no* agent promote or list your property. An agent doesn't want to put effort into something he or she will most likely not be paid for.

Not all agents are similarly motivated, and just because they've been an agent for a long time doesn't automatically make them the best agent for your needs.

TRUE LIFE STORY

After purchasing a home that needed some work, I asked the agent who'd sold it to me whether she knew of any more houses in the area that also needed work. Her response?

"Well, I can set you up to receive e-mail listings." Wow, don't put yourself out. I didn't take her up on her offer.

At the time, I was in my early thirties. I had just paid cash for a home in an era when everyone else was financing. I was asking for more properties, and presumably, she understood that I could pay cash for those as well. This wasn't some $15,000 property either. This property was six figures—easily in the midrange of properties in the area.

Yes, I made a low offer, but the seller accepted it over other offers, and I closed the deal. Yet when I asked the agent for more, she was unwilling to do anything that resembled work to help me find more deals.

I never did another deal with that agent again. Instead, I found a more responsive agent who was more interested in helping me buy houses.

Agents are not all the same, so make sure you're choosing the right agent for yourself.

LOWBALL OFFERS

You may get an offer that is too low to please you. This is called a lowball offer, and while it may make you angry, don't overreact.

You do not have to accept a lowball offer. In fact, you don't have to do anything with it, but I recommend countering the offer with one of your own. The prospective buyer doesn't have to accept it either, but closing the door on the conversation is never a good idea.

TRUE LIFE STORY

One time, the first offer I received on a house I was selling was extremely low. I was tempted to tell the buyers to just take a hike, but instead I called their agent and explained that we were too far apart on price, and we wouldn't be responding to their offer.

She urged me to counter and let me know that this was a starter offer and that the buyers were willing to go higher.

We went back and forth with the buyers, and on three separate occasions, I told the agent we were too far apart to continue negotiations. This was not as a ploy on my part but because the offers were simply too low for us to accept. They ultimately increased their offer to an acceptable level, but if we had simply ignored their original offer, we may have lost out on the sale altogether.

Don't take it personally if you receive a really rotten offer. Counter it and see what happens.

CHAPTER 14
Listing Options

FOR SALE BY OWNER

It is supremely tempting to try to sell your home yourself. You are not required by law to use an agent to sell your home and sellers pay real estate agents around 6 percent of the entire sales price. That's not small potatoes! Selling it by yourself is a valid, legal way to sell your home.

However, statistics show that homes that are for sale by owner, or FSBO, take longer to sell and end up selling for less money. Buyers see that the home is being sold without an agent and feel they should be getting a discounted price.

While you may wish to sell your home yourself, not all houses make good FSBO properties.

TRUE LIFE STORY

On a recent visit to friends in Florida, my husband and I went for a walk. Their neighborhood backs up to a gated community, and our walk took us through that neighborhood as well. As with any subdivision, there were a few houses on the market, but what really surprised me were the number of properties listed FSBO.

While FSBO is legal, a successful sale by owner is dependent on several factors, not the least of which is drive-by traffic. There is very little drive-by traffic in a gated community. In fact, the very reason for the gate is to keep nonresidents out of the neighborhood.

Dead-end streets offer similarly low drive-by traffic, as do remote locations.

Potential buyers viewing other houses listed in the neighborhood would pass these homes and may even ask their agents for more information, but your buyer pool is significantly limited in a gated community, in small towns, and on dead-end streets.

Further complicating the sale is whether you offer commission to a buyer's agent. A real estate agent is required by law to show buyers any home they wish to see, regardless of whether there is a commission offered. However, there is no law that states in what order these homes must be shown. Agents not being offered a commission will not be enthusiastic to show your home, and most certainly will not make it a priority.

Next, consider the actual home. Odd houses are harder to sell than more traditional homes, even *with* a real estate agent. Unique is a four-letter word in real estate. Very few people are looking for a geodesic dome or a house with nine bedrooms. Unusual features—such as a pool in an area where pools are not common (think Illinois or Minnesota)—also make your home more difficult to sell, as your buyer pool is significantly smaller.

I was fortunate to once live in Madison, Wisconsin, where the FSBO idea had not only caught hold but also had been so successful that the largest listing agency in the area was FSBOMadison.com.

There are similar sites other major cities now, too. In many of these cities, it is not weird to sell your property yourself, but not very many communities have embraced this concept.

However, when a home is not listed on the MLS, it does not rack up days on market, so if you aren't rushed, there isn't a significant downside to trying out FSBO first.

PROS

Save on costs

I had sold two houses by myself before I was licensed. Both were difficult to sell to begin with. One had an in-ground pool in an area where in-ground pools were extremely uncommon. The other was a lakefront property, a home that was much more expensive than the rest of the homes in the surrounding area.

I saved more than $25,000 by selling them myself. That's a lot of money. You can't dispute that dollar figure. I kept that money in my pocket instead of giving it to someone else, and I don't regret it. The extra work I had to do to sell the houses was not nearly worth $25,000, so I was happy with my decision.

You have more control over the sale

When I sold these houses myself, I controlled the sale, I controlled the negotiations, and I felt no pressure to accept any of the offers until I got the price I was looking for. Neither home was a rushed sale, both times we were moving because we wanted to, and my husband worked from home, so there was absolutely no pressure to sell in any particular time frame.

The lake house went through nine rounds of negotiations—and twice I told the buyer's agent, "We are too far apart on price. I don't think this is going to work out."

She insisted on continuing negotiations, and we eventually came to an agreement on price after the buyers finally raised their offer considerably. I felt no pressure to accept their low offer and didn't care if they walked away, which is the best position to be in.

I got the impression their agent was pushing them very hard to increase their offer. Not everyone is as comfortable with negotiation as I am. If you are selling the property yourself, be willing to walk away. And remember: Don't take lowball offers personally, since this is just business.

CONS

Unfortunately, not everything is unicorns and rainbows when it comes to selling your home yourself.

There is a statistically lower selling price

There is no getting around the fact that homes sold without an agent sell for less money, take longer to close, and have a general stigma against them.

Sellers primarily list and sell properties themselves to avoid paying a sales commission, so buyers are expecting a seller who is distressed or even cheap. Buyers expect to save money on an FSBO listing because the seller isn't paying a commission.

According to statistics from Realtor.com, homes listed without an agent sell for up to 15 percent less compared to sellers that used an agent. While real estate commissions vary from state to state, I have seen commissions around 5.5–6 percent of the sales price. Right off the bat, you have shot yourself in the foot. It's likely better for you to lose the 6 percent than to risk losing 15 percent.

Add to that the extra time it typically takes to sell by yourself and the lower exposure to buyers because your property isn't listed on the MLS, and you can start to understand why real estate agents can be a much better choice.

It takes longer to sell

Most buyers use a real estate agent to help them find a house and walk them through the purchase process—especially first timers. There's just so much people don't know about the process of buying a home.

The first things a good agent does are make sure his or her buyers are qualified to buy a house and determine what their price range is. After gathering this information, the agent will turn to the MLS, type criteria into the system, and pull up a list of properties that meet the buyers' needs.

If your home is not on that list, buyers most likely won't even know about it. They would have to drive past it or find it on Craigslist or some other site you've advertised it on to find the listing. Few buyers viewing your property means that it will take much longer to sell. Add in a path-less-traveled street or a cooler market, and you're looking at some significant time on the market.

I have no doubt that it took me longer to sell these houses than if they had been listed with a traditional agent. Fortunately, I was not in a time crunch, which made the FSBO option appropriate for my situation.

You're showing it yourself

On top of a home's taking longer to sell and selling for less money, you also have to show the property yourself. This presents a problem: Buyers don't want you there during the showing. They want to feel free to discuss the pros and cons of the home without fear of being overheard. So how do you let them into the house without being there?

If they are not being represented by an agent, you will have to be at the home to let them in, but you should plan on leaving once they have arrived. It doesn't matter whether you are selling by yourself or with an agent: Buyers do not feel comfortable with your being in the home. Once you let them in, make yourself scarce.

If they are being represented by an agent, get a lockbox on the front door and be gone before they arrive. The agent will take care of showing the property. Do not give the code to the buyers themselves; share the door code only with the agent.

There's less exposure to buyers

Most buyers use a real estate agent to help them find a house. Agents have MLS access, which is where they find listings to share with their clients. If you're not an agent, you will not have access to the MLS.

You'll face an uphill battle trying to connect with buyers if you aren't advertising where they're looking.

Agents are telling their buyers about properties listed on the MLS only.

HIRE AN ATTORNEY

If you are not being represented by a real estate agent in your transaction, you should absolutely hire a real estate attorney to help guide you through the process. Note: I said real estate attorney. An attorney who specializes in other types of law may not be familiar with all aspects of real estate law. While the attorney may still represent you, he or she may not be as up-to-date as an attorney who practices solely real estate law. Get an attorney who specifically practices real estate law.

Contracts are complicated

Contracts are written in legalese, and a word in the regular English vernacular can mean something quite different in legalese written in a real estate contract. Once both parties sign a contract, it becomes binding, regardless of whether or not you understand everything.

Have your attorney review the language of the contract before you sign it—and explain anything you don't understand. Also have your attorney approve any addendums, requests, continuances, and so on, after you are under contract—again, *before* you sign it.

In the case of multiple offers on your home, your attorney can review each one with you so you can compare apples to apples.

Make sure all rights are transferred correctly

There are so many blanks to be filled in on a contract. Colorado's contract is currently seventeen pages long. Every time the Real Estate Commission changes the contract, I take an eight-hour class to learn the best way to fill out the contract to represent my client's best interests—and to learn how to counter a contract that is not written in my client's best interests.

I'll go out on a limb and guess that you have not taken this class. Are you paying a "normal amount" for property taxes owed for the years you have owned the property, or is the buyer requesting an unreasonable sum? How do you even know what a "normal amount" is?

Is the buyer asking you to pay for things a buyer would typically cover? If you're new to the game, all these little charges can start to add up. A real estate agent is not the only person who can look out for your best interests, so if you decide to go it alone, don't go it completely alone. Hire a competent real estate attorney.

FLAT-FEE BROKER

Another listing option is a flat-fee broker. With this type of broker, you pay the real estate agent a predetermined amount (a flat fee) to list your home on the MLS rather than paying the traditional percentage of the sales price. On a $200,000 home, the typical 6 percent commission is $12,000. In this case, a flat-fee broker might charge only $1,500. Remember that in a traditional payment, that $12,000 is split between the buyer's agent and the seller's agent involved in the sale. The $1,500 for a flat-fee broker would go to the seller's agent for listing the property and does not include any payment for the buyer's agent.

There are two subsets of this approach. First, there is the flat-fee agent who lists your home on the MLS for you but then does no additional work. As the seller, you handle the showings, you handle the negotiations, and you make sure the timeline is followed and all the deadlines are met. Alternatively, there is the flat-fee yet full-service agent who helps with negotiation and everything else a traditional agent does. This second model is gaining in popularity, although slowly. This approach regularly runs around $2,500, higher than the cost of a discounted flat-fee broker but still far less than that of the traditional commission-based service. Remember that in this model, the $2,500 goes to the listing agent only and you still have to pay the buyer's agent, since the seller traditionally pays the fee for both sides of the transaction.

This best-of-both-worlds approach gives you the freedom to negotiate directly with your buyer while saving a significant portion of the commission you would otherwise pay to a listing agent.

While this sounds amazing (I've sold homes this way too), you run the risk of alienating other full-service agents by not using them or one of their peers. Legally, real estate agents are required to put their client's needs first and to show any home the client wants to see—regardless of commission offered to the agents. The stigma related to flat-fee brokers could not only cause trouble for your relationship with agents in the future, it could make selling your home more challenging.

However, agents are not bound to show properties in any particular order, and many agents will put these lower-commission properties, or ones listed with a flat-fee brokerage, at the bottom of the list of homes to be shown. Typically, before the agent gets around to showing your property, their buyer could have already fallen in love with a different house.

TRUE LIFE STORY

I had an agent I bought a property from, tell me that he would not show properties listed FSBO or with flat-fee agents because they do not support the industry. While I get where he is coming from, I didn't use him after that purchase because I didn't feel he had my best interests in mind.

Selling by owner and using a flat-fee broker are both valid, legal ways to sell your home. However, according to a survey by Realtor. com, 89 percent of sellers are using an agent to list their homes, so keep that in mind when deciding how best to sell your home.

CHAPTER 15

Competitive Pricing

Now that you've decided how you are going to list your home, you must choose a price.

If you are using an agent, he or she will recommend a price range based on similar properties that have recently sold in your area.

Let's talk about Zillow and their Zestimate. Note the word is *estimate* with a Z thrown onto the front for fun. Many sellers—and buyers, too—check the price of the home against the Zestimate on Zillow. A home listed significantly higher or lower than the Zestimate can appear to be either a steal or overpriced when it is actually listed very close to market price.

PRO·TIP   *A Zestimate is not an appraisal. It is an estimate, and it can be spot-on or wildly inaccurate.*

Take, for example, the home of Zillow's CEO, Spencer Rascoff. His home was reportedly sold for $1.05 million yet had a Zestimate of $1.75 million—a discrepancy of almost 40 percent!

A real estate attorney in northern Illinois filed a lawsuit against Zillow because the Zestimate of her home was about 10 percent lower than what she believed to be the true market value. Buyers balked at her price, citing Zillow's Zestimate.

Zillow has repeatedly stated that the Zestimate is not an appraisal but merely an estimate of market value based on recent sales extrapolated using their proprietary formula. Your agent should be able to give you a better, more accurate estimate of where to list your home, based on recent sales of comparable properties that may or may not coincide with the Zestimate. Use the numbers your agent provides.

When reviewing the comparable properties list (comps), discount the odd ducks—both high and low outliers. Low comps can mean the sellers had to get out quickly and couldn't wait around for a full-price offer. Comps coming in too high could have concessions included in the deal that made the sales price appear higher.

For example, the last house that I sold appears to have a higher sales price than what was actually received because the buyers did not have the cash to cover the closing costs. They requested $5,000 in seller concessions to be used toward closing costs. I was already losing money on the sale of this house and did not want to take an additional $5,000 hit, so I agreed to the terms of their offer but increased the price by $5,000. This essentially rolled their closing cost concessions into their loan. The buyers agreed, the house appraised at the higher amount, and I walked out with what I needed. Everyone was happy, but the home looks as though it sold for $5,000 more.

INCITING A BIDDING WAR

Best way to start a bidding war? List your home at a lower price than what you expect it to sell for, solely to instigate a bidding war.

This is a pricing strategy that I absolutely hate. I think that when you list your home, you should be willing to accept an offer at that price—meaning that if your home is worth $500,000 but you price it at $450,000 just to generate interest, you should also be willing to accept an offer of $450,000.

It is disingenuous to price it significantly below market just to gain more attention, more offers, and a bidding war. On the other hand, this is a fairly effective strategy, especially in a hot market and especially if the property hovers around a significant psychological price marker. Fellow agents of mine shared that this is how everyone lists homes in their respective areas. Actually, they say that listing at the price you expect people to pay is a bad thing, as you will not hit the people you're aiming for with this strategy. Talk to your agent if you have questions about this strategy, as he or she will know the local market and can give you advice that best fits your situation.

BE WARY OF OVERPRICING

The number one reason a property does not sell is price. A home does not sell for its listing price simply because that is the price the seller wants. It sells for what it's worth in today's market, which is influenced by many things, not the least of which is what other properties have recently sold for. The amount of money you have invested in a home is immaterial to the price the home will sell for, and basing your pricing strategy on this number can hurt your sale.

For example, say you purchased your home for $100,000 and then put in $50,000 in improvements and upgrades. You now have $150,000 invested in your home. If similar homes in the area are selling for $130,000, you're not going to get $150,000 for your home. House prices and appraisals are based on what similar homes nearby have recently sold for.

If houses near you are showing sale prices around $130,000, the fact that you have put $50,000 into the property has absolutely no relevance. It will most likely sell for around $130,000 because that is what it is worth. If you're priced significantly higher than the comps are, you will need to reduce your price to be more in line with the market.

If you are using an agent, listen to his or her recommendations and ask what led to the price suggestion. Your agent should use the term *comps* when explaining the reasoning, and if he or she does not, you may want to consider a different agent to help you sell.

If you are not using an agent, gathering up recently sold properties can be a much more arduous task. Cookie-cutter subdivisions make this a lot easier. You can also pay a real estate agent for a broker's price opinion, commonly known as a BPO. This will usually run less than $200 and is literally the agent's opinion of the market and where you should list your home.

You could pay for an appraisal, but be aware that the buyer's bank will not use this appraisal to value the home. Getting an appraisal does not benefit buyers in any way, and they will not reimburse you for this expense. An appraisal will run closer to $400.

But as I have said before and will say again, pricing the property too high will cause it to sit, gathering market time and turning stale. Meanwhile, more appropriately priced properties pop up, get shown, go under contract, and sell. You can either take your property off the market or reduce the price significantly to try to overcome the stigma—but pricing too high does more harm than good.

PSYCHOLOGICAL BARRIERS

As I have said before, your agent should give you a price range in which to list your home, based on the prices that similar properties in your area have sold for in recent months. While it is tempting to go for the high end of the range, there are a few things to consider.

What, precisely, is the range given? If your agent is recommending a price range that crosses a major psychological barrier, such as $200,000, going lower will ultimately help your sale.

Consider this: Buyers have a price range. A range of $175,000 to $200,000 isn't uncommon, and smart buyers' agents may even bump the range to $205,000 just to capture the properties listed slightly above. But what if your buyer doesn't have a smart agent?

Listing at $199,900 is really close to $200,000, without going over the barrier and possibly eliminating potential buyers for a mere extra $100. If you shoot for the high end of your agent's suggested of $195,000 to $205,000, you stand to lose a lot of potential buyers for very little monetary gain. This is a simple exercise in psychological management.

PROBLEMS WITH AGENT COMMISSIONS

An agent is compensated only when a property sells. Using a 5 percent commission, a property that sells for $100,000 will gross $5,000 in commissions. Split this between two agents (buyer and seller), that is $2,500 each. If the home sells for $105,000, that same 5 percent commission increases to a whopping $5,250, or $2,625 for either side. While this is an additional $5,000 to you, the higher sales price nets the agents almost nothing else. But negotiating the higher price comes with the risk of losing the sale entirely, all for an extra $125 to the agent.

This doesn't even take into account that commissions are typically split between the agent you are working with and his or her employing broker. Many times, the split is fifty/fifty, meaning that extra $125 really turns into an extra $62.50. This is hardly worth risking the entire sale.

PRO·TIP *Real estate agents simply aren't incentivized to get you the highest sales price. Consider offering your agent a bonus for securing sales prices of over a certain amount.*

CHAPTER 16

Pre-inspecting Your Home

A pre-inspection occurs when you, the seller, have an inspector come out and examine your home before you put it on the market.

It is almost guaranteed that your buyer will have an inspection, so if you get your home inspected beforehand, you'll know everything that's wrong with the house and be able to eliminate surprises during the sale, right? Maybe, maybe not. While it sounds like an awesome idea, it has its pros and cons.

PROS

You can fix anything that may be an issue

Deal-breaker items such as a broken foundation, mold growth, or a leaking roof can be caught and fixed before you are in a binding contract. If you repair an issue, it no longer needs to be disclosed (see chapter eight on disclosing for my advice about disclosing everything). Everyone knows that things break in houses, but knowing that there's something wrong before purchasing can be distracting to buyers. Repairing problems ahead of time can increase your negotiating power later, during the inspection.

Having a home that passes an inspection with a few minor issues (inspectors always find *something!*) is reassuring to buyers that they're making the right decision, which makes the contract far more likely to go through.

There will be fewer surprises after you're under contract

You have already had the home inspected by a licensed inspector and presumably have repaired most of the issues identified. Knowing that the home inspection won't turn up much, if anything, can give you peace of mind that your contract is solid and will close on schedule.

Your buyer may forgo an inspection altogether

This really is the top reason to get your home inspected before you list it. There is a decent chance that your buyers will skip their inspection altogether—you've already done one and presumably fixed anything that was found. Why waste the money on another inspection that will show nothing?

If your inspection turns up relatively few items or nothing serious and you have receipts for the repairs that you needed to make, you can share this with the buyers to help nudge them in the direction of no inspection.

CONS

Of course, there are cons to getting a home inspection before you put your home on the market. A pre-inspected home does not guarantee that the property is in fantastic shape. It's a snapshot of the condition of the home at the time of the inspection.

I would *never* allow my clients to go with just a seller's inspection report. I would insist they get their own—or sign a fantastic waiver that states they do not hold the agent responsible for any issues that come up with the home, since they willingly proceeded without the inspection.

There may be inconsistent inspections

There is no guarantee the buyers' inspector will find the same things that your inspector did. Home inspectors are human, which means they are prone to mistakes just like anyone else. Perhaps your inspector missed something, or something stops working between the time you had your inspection and the buyers have theirs. Maybe you chose an inspector who is more relaxed about the small stuff, and their inspector is the opposite.

A home inspector has a unique ability to make small things seem enormous—especially to newer buyers. On the flip side, an inspector can also make a larger issue sound not so bad. Perhaps he or she mentions an issue to you, and you brush it off assuming it's not that big a deal.

If you do decide to have your home pre-inspected, make sure you schedule the inspection during a time when you are available to go through the home with the inspector. Ask questions until you understand the severity of the issues and the approximate costs to get them fixed. While an inspector isn't going to give you an ironclad quote, he or she is usually familiar with general prices and can advise whether an issue requires a $10 or $10,000 fix.

You are paying money out of pocket

Paying for a home inspection is going to take money out of your pocket that could be a waste. If your home is in tip-top shape and your inspector finds nothing amiss, you may feel as if you've wasted your money.

Of course, if your initial home inspection brought up many issues that you fixed, that may have been worth your time and money. You may have saved a deal that wasn't even in place yet, simply because the buyers' inspector didn't find as many issues.

DIY HOME INSPECTIONS

I've never had a home pre-inspected. My clients didn't want to spend the money, and the personal residences I've sold had all been recently rehabbed, so I knew everything was up-to-date, up to code, and brand-new.

Here is a pre-inspection checklist to help you gauge the condition of your home. Note: Not all items will apply to all homes.

General

- [ ] **Windows:** Check that they open and close easily. Any broken panes?
- [ ] **Doors:** Check that they open and close completely. Do they stick? Lock? Scrape the floor at any point?
- [ ] **Floors:** Any creaking? Obvious unevenness? You can fix wood-floor creaking with baby powder between the joints (it acts as a lubricant) or by going beneath the floor with a few well-placed screws.
- [ ] **Walls:** Any holes?
- [ ] **Trim:** Any damage or missing pieces? Animals can be brutal to wood trim, and matching old trim is almost impossible.
- [ ] **Lights:** Turn on every light switch to make sure it works.
- [ ] **Stairs:** Walk up and down the stairs and touch all the spindles on the railing. Do they seem sturdy or wobbly? Do the stairs creak? Are any parts missing?
- [ ] **Outlets:** Get a voltage tester at your local big-box home improvement store for less than $20 and test every single outlet.
- [ ] **Furnace:** Look at the furnace. Are there any stickers that indicate installation date? When was the last time you changed the filter? If you can't remember, go get a new one.
- [ ] **Water heater:** Any stickers on this to indicate installation date? Check for water around the base of the water heater. If you see water near the water heater, your buyer's inspector will too. This can be an indication that it is failing and you should replace it. (Although I've never had one slow leak. Mine are always working, then completely fail.)

Kitchen

- [ ] **Cabinets/drawers:** Open all cabinets and drawers, then close them again. Do they move smoothly? Does anything prevent any of the doors or drawers from easy use?

- ☐ **Oven:** Open and inspect the oven. Does the door open slowly, indicating the springs still work? What is the condition of the oven? Cleaning the oven is a quick task yet speaks volumes about how you care for the home.
- ☐ **Stove:** Turn on each burner on the stove. If it is a gas stove, turn each burner on and off individually before turning the next one on to make sure they all turn on by themselves rather than catching the flame from an adjacent burner. If they all work individually, turn them all on to make sure they all work at the same time. If you have electric, just turn all the burners on at once.
- ☐ **Fridge:** Open the refrigerator and freezer doors. Do they open easily?
- ☐ **Dishwasher:** Open and inspect the dishwasher. Do the springs work on the dishwasher door?
- ☐ **Garbage disposal:** Does the garbage disposal run? (Don't forget to turn on the water before you test it.)
- ☐ **Cabinet interiors:** Take a good look at the cabinets. Are they in good shape? Do the bottoms look grungy and gross? Do the hinges work smoothly?
- ☐ **Microwave:** Open the microwave and take a peek inside. Unless you cleaned it yesterday, give it a good scrub.
- ☐ **Range hood:** Turn on the range hood fan and light to make sure they work. Peek underneath to check for filth—this is a commonly overlooked area for cleaning.
- ☐ **Stone countertops:** Check for chips and cracks.
- ☐ **Formica countertops:** Check for chips.
- ☐ **Tile:** Check the floor for cracked tiles.
- ☐ **Windows:** Open and close all windows.

Bathrooms
- ☐ **Plumbing/drainage:** Flush the toilet. Fill up the sink and tub and then let the water run out to test for backups or poorly performing drains. Check for leaks from all faucets.
- ☐ **Floors:** Any broken tiles?

- ☐ **Toilet:** Does it rock instead of sitting solidly on the floor?
- ☐ **Tub:** Any cracks or chips?
- ☐ **Vanity:** Check the condition. Make sure to open it and check the inside too.
- ☐ **Ventilation:** Does the fan work? Is there a window? Does it open and close easily?

Bedrooms
- ☐ **Closets:** Do closets have doors? Do they open and close easily?
- ☐ **Windows:** Open and close all windows.
- ☐ **Floors:** Check the state of the flooring. Does the carpet have stains, worn spots, and so on? Is the hardwood scratched and damaged?

Living/Dining/Family Room
- ☐ **Doors:** Any doors? Do they open and close easily?
- ☐ **Floors:** What is the state of the flooring?
- ☐ **Walls:** Are there any holes or other damage to the walls?
- ☐ **Windows:** Do the windows work?

Basement
- ☐ **Odor:** What does it smell like? An overpowering odor can be mold or mildew.
- ☐ **Walls:** Do the walls have any cracks? Small, hairline cracks are not so concerning, but large cracks—especially horizontal cracks—can be an indicator of bigger foundation problems.

Exterior
- ☐ **Sprinkler:** Turn on the sprinkler system.
- ☐ **Lights:** Turn them on. Do all the bulbs work, or do you need to replace some?
- ☐ **Outlets:** Test them.
- ☐ **Fence:** Walk the fence to check for loose boards and overall sturdiness.
- ☐ **Siding:** What is the condition of the siding?

- ☐ **Roof:** Go to the south side of the house and look at the shingles. The south side gets the most sun, and curling or buckling can be an indication that the roof needs work.
- ☐ **Garage door:** Does it open and close easily?
- ☐ **Lawn:** What does the grass look like?
- ☐ **Yard:** Are there any dead trees/shrubs?

Taking stock of the home can help you decide on a price as well. You may not have noticed the cracked siding in the back of the home if you've never walked back there, or the window that doesn't open may be in a room you don't often use. Walk the entire house and take note of what you want to fix and what you're fine leaving alone. I cannot stress this enough, though. If you know something is broken and do not intend to repair it, disclose the defect.

CHAPTER 17

Listing Your House on the MLS

As previously noted, your agent should have access to the most popular MLS service in your area. Once your home is listed on the MLS, ask your agent to send you the listing, and read it carefully to make sure it says what you want it to say.

Double-check that all the information is correct in the system. The numbers on a keyboard are close together, and agents are human. It's easy to fat-finger the number of bedrooms or bathrooms on a listing. While it's an easy mistake to make, it can cause your listing to sit on the market if not corrected quickly.

After you have read through the description and made sure all the stats of the house are correct, click through the photos to make sure they are pictures of *your* home and that they are in the correct order. You want a picture of the exterior of the home to be first and subsequent pictures to be in a logical order. Kitchen, living areas, and bedrooms before bathrooms. You do not want your first image to be of a toilet.

I was viewing a listing in my area to keep up with the local offerings and noticed the recently rehabbed home's listing had images of the original kitchen in the mix. I had seen the home both pre- and post-remodel, and it was confusing that the sellers had included the original kitchen images with no comments about them.

I sent the agent a note, but the old images were never taken down. That won't happen on my listings, because I am extremely conscientious about them. Make sure it doesn't happen on your listing either.

Broker's remarks are a hidden section of many MLS systems—hidden from the public view. It is a place for listing agents to convey to the showing agents special details such as "cat is on premises—please don't let him out." Or "special needs child lives in home, showings available only eight to eleven and three to six." Essentially, information that doesn't necessarily pertain to the actual home but still needs to be shared with other agents.

If you have special showing instructions or specific information you want conveyed to the agents who will be showing your home, ask your agent to put them in the broker's remarks and ask him or her to show these to you so you can double-check them for accuracy.

Cooperating sites

The MLS isn't the only site your listing should appear on. There are many sites that share MLS information, and you never know where buyers might be looking—either before or after they connect with an agent.

The websites change daily, so ask your agent for a list of all the sites your home will be listed on besides the MLS.

WHEN SHOULD YOU LIST?

If you have the luxury of wanting to move instead of needing to move, listing your home during certain times of the year will get more eyeballs on the property and more feet through the door, simply because more people are searching for a home at that time.

You may have heard the term *spring selling season*. The highest number of buyers are looking in the spring. Depending on where you're located, early February to late March is the prime listing time. Home buyers with school-age children are looking to finalize their purchase and get settled into their new home between the time school ends in spring and before school starts up again in the fall. Even home buyers without school-age children know that the most houses will be on the market during the spring, giving them the most options.

Just before Thanksgiving through New Year's Day is the worst time to try to sell your home. In fact, many sellers who have not yet sold their property will take it off the market during the holiday season.

If you can't wait until spring to put your home on the market, all is not lost. You just need to make extra sure that your property looks, smells, and shows great!

PRESALE AND POCKET LISTING

Perhaps you aren't excited about the prospect of tons of people traipsing through your house. If you have chosen a real estate agent to list your home, ask him or her to shop the property around the office first, before it goes live on the MLS. If someone in the office has the perfect person to buy your home, you can save a lot of showing time by having just one person walk through.

While this is no guarantee the buyer will make an offer, you could avoid a lot of hassle by offering it to someone before it is officially on the market. Please note, this scenario does not typically generate the highest offer for the home, but if privacy is more of a concern than top dollar, this is a viable solution.

Presale and pocket listings are similar but different. The presale has the agent shopping the listing around *before* it is listed on the MLS, while the pocket listing has the agent shopping it around *instead of* listing it on the MLS.

My state commission has been cracking down on this practice, on the grounds that if this is the agent's idea, it may be unfair to the seller. However, it is perfectly legal, especially if the idea comes from the seller!

TOP TIPS FOR HOME PHOTOGRAPHY

There is a lot of advice bandied about on the Internet. The "Do It Yourself" crowd has just as loud a voice as the "Hire a Professional" group.

Whenever I sell a house, my husband takes the pictures. This is true with both our personal residences and the homes I list for clients. Why? Because he's just as good as a professional photographer, but he's free to me. My husband takes excellent pictures. He spends time lining up the shot, adjusting the lights and furniture, and takes about twenty-five shots in each position so we have plenty of images to choose from. He also spends a good deal of time in the home and takes pictures at different times of the day to see which light best captures each room. Sometimes an afternoon shot looks great for one room, while a morning shot works better for another room.

Now, if I had to personally take the pictures, it would be extremely apparent that my amateur self was taking them. I'm not a good photographer, so I don't personally provide this service. But I choose my husband to take the pictures because I know his quality is excellent. I really hate scrolling through listing pictures that look as if the agents took them themselves using the original iPhone camera.

I've seen a ton of listings in which the images were obviously taken at weird angles and with funky camera lenses to make the house appear different. I don't even understand why this is a thing. The house will not magically conform to the way the images appear. You can't make a house look bigger in real life than it actually is, yet you can absolutely make it look bigger than real life in images. So, potential buyers make appointments to see your home, only to walk away disappointed and with no offer on the table.

You want buyers that are truly uninterested in your home based on the images alone to dismiss your home before they ever walk through the door, saving you the time and hassle. Get the qualified, truly-interested-in-your-property-the-way-it-is buyers through the door by providing reality-based photography in your listing.

It costs you *nothing* to take some pictures yourself to see whether you like the way they look. Get your agent's opinion on the quality of the images, and if you aren't sure about them, ask some friends.

Take pictures at three different times during the day

If it's your house, you can set up the shot and just keep coming back and taking pictures as the light changes. Take multiple pictures each time, and move your position a little to get slightly different angles. You're taking these shots with your digital camera, and it doesn't cost you anything more to take one hundred than it does to take one or even ten.

Lighting plays a huge role in photography, and not all rooms will photograph best in the same light. I have had listings in which the living room looked best at night, while the kitchen looked best photographed during the day. It didn't look weird that the house was obviously shot at different times, and most important, the images were an accurate representation of the home.

For shots of the exterior, aim for the golden hour—the period right after sunrise or right before sunset. Outdoor photos look best when taken during the golden hour.

Take accurate pictures

It is so frustrating to view images of a home online and then get to the house to find it's *nothing* like the pictures you've seen. Again, wide-angle lenses may get people into your home, but misrepresentations won't keep them there, and they certainly won't do anything to get them to write an offer.

The point of online images is to show potential buyers what your home looks like. Not all buyers are going to like your home, so if it's not for them, screen them out of the equation before they even get to your house. Don't try to trick them into coming to see a home they would have otherwise written off.

You're going to have plenty of showings that go nowhere. Don't let your images misrepresent your house. I still remember going to one home and seeing a supposed bedroom in the online images, but saw something completely different in real life. I actually was on the floor trying to figure out what angle the owners had taken the picture from—it was that far off from reality. I even went home and looked at the pictures again. No, I wasn't going to buy the house, but I was really curious to see how they made a five-foot tall nook under the stairs look like a full-sized bedroom.

Having nice photos of your house doesn't actually change your house. If you misrepresent the property by manipulating the images, you aren't going to get a sale. You're just going to make the potential buyers annoyed. Show the home the way it is, warts and all.

Pay for photography if necessary

Not everyone is going to be a great photographer. Even armed with these tips and all the time and test shots in the world, you could be jumping over dollars to save nickels if your images look unprofessional.

PRO·TIP *Ultimately, you want your home to show in the best light. Make sure your images are the best, most accurate representation of your home.*

If DIY appeals to you, spend some extra time when taking your own photos.

If your agent offers to take pictures for you, ask to see examples of other homes he or she has photographed. If the pics look good, give them a go. Do not be afraid to tell your agent that you'd rather hire out a photographer, though! Don't use photos that look bad just to save a buck.

THE LISTING

Your listing should not leave anything to the buyer's imagination. It should give any and all pertinent information about your house. You want people to read it and say, "That's not the house for me." Why? Because showing a house is a pain in the butt. You have to clean everything up—no small feat if you have kids—and leave the house during the entire showing.

The point of listing a house isn't to get the most feet through the door; the point of listing the house is to sell the house. You want the most qualified people walking through the door as few times as possible so you don't have to deal with it for an extended period of time. There is no prize for having 500 showings with no offers.

Other things to include in your listing are actual room dimensions. I *hate* when the room sizes aren't included in the listing. Again, this goes back to those unrealistic photos. If you include the room sizes, then people will know that your master bedroom is actually twelve by fifteen feet instead of the twenty-four by thirty-six feet that it appears in the images. Also, giving them actual measurements makes it a lot easier to visualize than the far less descriptive "huge master bedroom."

Note who took the measurements in the listing, as well, and always include the caveat "Measurements taken by homeowner [or whoever actually measured the property] and are considered to be approximate. Buyer to confirm all measurements." This prevents the buyer from coming back and accusing you of misrepresentation if their measurements are different from yours. However, make your measurements as accurate as possible. Again, you want to show the house to someone who wants to buy it, not someone who thinks it's way different from it is.

Sellers should also include in the listing any homeowners' association (HOA) restrictions such as pets or strict rental policies. It would most certainly be a deal breaker for your home to be put under contract by bullmastiff enthusiasts only to discover that there is a thirty-pound weight limit on pets. The contract would be broken, and you'd add some unnecessary market time to your listing. If you would have included the pet size restrictions in the listing, those bullmastiff enthusiasts wouldn't even have looked at your house, knowing they couldn't have their dogs with them.

If your association does not allow rentals, post that in the listing, too, so you can avoid the investor buyers who are looking only for places they can rent out. If the association allows a certain number of rentals, find out how many units are being rented. Again, avoid the disappointed investors who break the contract when they discover they can't rent it out because the property or complex is already at rental capacity.

Do you have any special tax breaks in place? If you're paying less in taxes because of a tax policy that benefits you but would most likely not benefit your buyer, state that. Again, you're looking for ways to make people say no to seeing your house. This gets the most targeted buyers through the door instead and wastes less of your time.

On the other hand, be sure to highlight any attributes that would make people want to see it—the point isn't to scare *everyone* off!

Does the property have any special features such as close proximity to an open space? If high-speed Internet or fiber optics is available, make that known. I have a friend who lives in rural Vermont, which is not a place normally associated with high-speed Internet. Luckily, the town offers high-speed Internet via a fiber-optic system. The local residents have learned how to run the lines because they could not get any Internet service in the area. Having high-speed Internet available in the middle of nowhere can put your property on the radar of someone who might otherwise ignore it.

The same should be said for any special transferable rates or offers. My city has its own fiber-optic service, and anyone who signed up during the first month it was offered has introductory rates forever! Not only that, but those rates can transfer to the next owner. The introductory rates are half the current rate, and prices are only going to go up. I've seen multiple listings in town highlight this feature.

If you have remodeled your home, there may be a big difference in the price that you purchased it for and your selling price. Note that the home was recently remodeled, and list the major improvements so buyers know why you're asking for the big price bump. This is especially important if you've owned the home for only a couple of years.

SELF-MARKETING

Once you've cleaned, decluttered, repaired, packed up, listed your home on the MLS, and double-checked the listing for accuracy and you're ready for buyers to walk through the door, you can really get down to business. Your agent is marketing your house in a multitude of ways, and you need to roll up your sleeves and pitch in too.

Are you on social media? Blast your listing on every social media platform you are on. Ask your friends, family, and followers to share, like, and retweet. You want to reach the maximum number of people, and you never know where your buyer is going to come from. Don't take the "that's my agent's job" attitude. It's your house, and you're the one who most wants to sell it and benefits most from it being sold. Do everything in your power to help it out. Plus, posting it on social media is free!

Did your agent provide you with flyers for buyers to take with them? Make sure they're exposed and easy to find. The kitchen counter is a popular spot for flyers. Have one framed next to the pile of takeaways in case the last one is taken before you can replenish.

Does your yard sign have a flyer box? If so, check it every day to be sure it's full.

Regarding yard signs, you need one. Unless your HOA is unbelievably restrictive and does not allow them, plant a sign in the middle of your yard, perpendicular to the street so people driving past from either side can see it. Your agent should provide you with a sign, and other agents are expecting to see one in the yard too. If your backyard is visible, or if you live on a corner lot, consider planting more than one sign.

CHAPTER 18

Preparing Your Home for Showings

Now that your house is listed on the MLS or you're selling it yourself, you're going to start having showings. Again, hot markets will have more showings more often, and slower markets may start well but will quickly dwindle off. In either market, you're going to need to be prepared for the viewings. The more prepared you keep your home, the less notice you'll need before a showing.

Here are some general things to do to prepare the home for listing and getting it ready to show:

LISTING UPGRADES AND REPAIRS

If your home has undergone significant changes since you purchased it, you may wish to consider listing all the upgrades you've performed with dates. While upgrading the doorknobs from 1980s shiny brass to the current trend of brushed nickel or oil-rubbed bronze isn't going to be a big deal to the buyer, the new furnace last year, the new water heater four years ago, and the new roof last month is absolutely worth mentioning. Any transferable warranties should also be noted.

This list does not have to be fancy or elaborate. A simple record of improvements and the dates completed will work just fine, especially for items that are not visible such as plumbing or electrical upgrades. If you had professionals perform the work, you may want to list that information as well.

Consider having this update list in a stand-alone frame so potential buyers can view it during their showing but can't take it with them. Try to condense it all into one page, but don't skip over important upgrades just to fit it all in. Get creative with the layout if you have more upgrades than space on a page, or use a larger frame.

Create a binder for the house with all the appliance manuals or manuals for items that are staying with the home. Write approximate installation dates on the manual for easy reference for the new owners too. Meticulous home records show potential buyers that you were on top of all maintenance.

NEIGHBORHOOD INFORMATION

Not everyone looking at your house is familiar with the area. Assume they are new, and show off your neighborhood with information inside a binder. Share favorite parts of where you live. Your enthusiasm for your area will shine through and make others want to live there too.

Schools

If your home is in a great school district—especially if it's located near a not-so-great district and there could be confusion. Note the elementary, middle, and high schools that occupants of your house could attend. Even if this information isn't important to you, it could nevertheless be very important to potential buyers.

Doing a little research on GreatSchools.org can give you talking points about the local schools if you don't have experience with them yourself.

Restaurants

A list of restaurants, bars, and dinner theaters in your area can show potential buyers that the area has a vibrant nightlife and offers many different things to do. Highlighting a few favorites from different culinary styles shows diversity in your area. Note any award-winning restaurants as well.

Local attractions

If your area is known for a specific local attraction, list it and include the distance to the attraction. If your area has multiple places people would like to go, list them all. The more, the better. I live near Rocky Mountain National Park, several ski resorts, a couple of iconic cities, and several local amusement parks and museums, and I list them all.

DRAWING ATTENTION TO DETAILS

In one house I sold, I had radiant heat beneath the tile in the bathrooms. The home was located in Wisconsin, so this was a real plus. However, this isn't something that's very noticeable to most buyers. The same is true for the upgraded electrical system, the laundry chute, and the kitchen pantry, as it was located behind a wall. A small note, printed on nice paper next to these items, will bring attention to the features.

If you have unusual but not readily apparent things in your home, such as a trash compactor, a wine cellar, a vacuum system, or even a dual flush toilet, a few cards can mean the difference between someone's choosing your home over another one—especially if you're in a cookie-cutter subdivision where there is little to differentiate one house from the next.

You never know what will push someone to your home instead of a different listing, so highlight anything that you believe sets your house apart. All is fair in love, war, and home selling.

ALWAYS BE PREPARED

Once your house is on the market, it needs to be clean every minute of the day for showings. If you do not normally make your bed every morning, acquire the habit. Have your children do the same.

Wipe the toothpaste out of the sink every single day. Put the toothbrush back in the holder and the toothpaste in the drawer, and wipe down the counters.

Pull the shower curtain closed, make sure the toilet has been flushed, and wipe anything off the mirror.

Open all window shades to let in natural light.

Put breakfast dishes in the dishwasher, and wipe down the counters. Do not leave dishes in a drying rack—put them away before you go.

Empty the wastebaskets and vacuum every other day to keep the house looking fresh and tidy.

Having a home neat and ready to show at a moment's notice means you can accept any showing request. You never know which buyer is going to be writing you an offer, so make sure each has the opportunity to see it.

Most agents send their clients listings, then schedule showings in a reasonable order, usually by geographic location. But frequently they drive past one home on their way to another and decide they want to see that one too. The ability to accommodate last-minute showings will only help you sell your home faster. In fact, the first day your home goes on the market is the day when you'll get the most showings. If you're in a hot market, your home will probably be booked with showings most of the day. Make plans to be out of the home for the entire day—and direct your agent to accept all showing requests for that day. If you're listing the home to hit the market on the weekend, plan to be out of the home the entire weekend. Maybe even take a short vacation to allow maximum showings.

LEAVE YOUR HOME DURING SHOWINGS

If you're selling with an agent, you should not be anywhere near the home during the showing—not sitting in the backyard, not walking around the block fifty times. Get in your car and leave the area. Grab a coffee at a local coffee shop, go grocery shopping, or just head to the library and read a magazine. Buyers do not feel comfortable discussing your house when you are there. Most likely, they will politely tour the property and leave quickly, striking it from their list.

No, really. Buyers do *not* want you at the house during showings. If you are selling FSBO and they have an agent representing them, leave the house during the showing. Do not think they want you to stay and show them all the neat stuff about your house. Do not think they want you hanging around to answer questions. They don't want you there.

If you are selling FSBO and they do not have an agent representing them, you may stay to welcome them into the home, tell them you'll be in the backyard if they have any questions, and ask them to let you know when they are finished. Then walk into the backyard and leave them alone. Read a book, tend to the garden, play with your kids, but do not stay inside the home. Buyers without agents still don't want a tour.

PRO·TIP *Under no circumstances should you be inside the house as a seller during the showing!*

Something else buyers don't want in the house during a showing? Your animals. If you have fish or a bird in a cage, that's different. The same goes for small lizards, gerbils, and so on. But if you have a large snake, strongly consider having it sleep over at a friend's house until you've sold your property. Snakes give most people the heebie-jeebies, and you're not going to persuade anyone to start loving snakes just because you've got one. Your scaly sidekick could make a potential buyer run right out of the house. Your eight-legged pets almost certainly will. (My sister-in-law used to have a pet tarantula—ugh.) Remember, the whole point of this exercise is to sell your house. You don't want to shoot yourself in the foot in an attempt to prove that snakes are great.

In fact, your dog should not be in the home during the showing either. It doesn't matter how cute he is or how well behaved. Some people are afraid of dogs, and others are allergic to them. Your dog isn't going to stay with the house anyway. Same with cats.

If you cannot take time off work to remove animals from the home during showings, consider hiring a pet sitter or asking a neighbor to come take them for an extended walk.

TRUE LIFE STORY

I will never forget the time I opened the door to a home with five large black Labs inside. I received no notice that the animals were in the home, nor did I know how to show the home to my clients with these giant dogs. They were friendly, but five dogs are five dogs, and black Labs are big. The clients did not even go inside the home.

On the more controversial side are the neighbor's dogs. Do you ask a neighbor with a loud dog to keep it inside during your showing? If potential buyers discover after they've bought the house next to the neighbor who leaves his giant canine outside to bark twenty-four hours, seven days a week, but you asked him to put it inside during your showings—could you be held liable?

TRUE LIFE STORY

Before I was an agent, I walked away from an otherwise perfect home precisely for this reason. As we walked up to the door to unlock it for the viewing, the neighbor's dog started barking so loud and so viciously, I was scared for my safety.

The fence was about a million years old and did nothing to bolster my confidence that I wasn't about to become a Scooby snack.

The home was amazing and had been on the market for several weeks in a market that did not allow homes to sit for long. I wondered why before I got to the home, but definitely not afterward, and made sure my agent told the seller that the dog next door was 100 percent the reason why I was not making an offer on the house.

As an agent, I open the lockbox on a home and get the key, then knock on the door and wait a moment to see whether anyone is home. I won't soon forget the woman who had just gotten out of her shower and answered the door wearing only a towel. "Can you come back in about thirty minutes? I'm not ready for you." I had arrived ten minutes *after* the appointment was scheduled to start.

We didn't make it back to her house. Those particular clients were from out of town and were on a tight schedule. Unless the homes are right next door to each other, I schedule my showings a half hour apart, so it's important to leave before the showing begins: We're in, we're out, and we're on to the next one. Typically, houses right next to each other won't be for sale at the same time, so once I've driven to the next property, your house has very little chance of being shown.

Don't sabotage your sale by being at the house—or worse, by being undressed—when your showing starts. Leave at least fifteen minutes before the showing is scheduled, just in case the buyer is running a bit early.

Your showing may also run late. Typically, this is because the buyer was either late or really likes your home and wants to spend more time looking around. Having the seller in the home makes the buyer uncomfortable—and you do not want to rush a potential sale. Leave early and return late.

When I was selling my last house, a buyer scheduled a showing later than I preferred. I had two small children who needed to go to bed about a half hour before the showing was scheduled to end, so I hoped the buyers wouldn't stay too long.

They ended up staying a half hour after the showing was supposed to end, and I had very cranky children the next day. But I also received an offer on my house. Definitely worth the crankiness, and I was glad I hadn't rushed them out of the home.

Give potential buyers all the time they need to explore your home without you. Making them uncomfortable by rushing them will give them a sense of unease about your home and will push them right out the door, never to return. Allow them to view the home on their own timeline by keeping the home ready to show at a moment's notice.

If you're an investor, this also applies to you. Don't hang around the house to show the potential buyers what improvements you've made. If you're selling a tenant-occupied home, make arrangements well in advance to have the tenants out of the property during the showing. You may have to incentivize your tenants to leave the property during showings. Money is an excellent incentive, and remember that having them home during the showing could cost you a lot more. Can you imagine a potential buyer walking into a messy house with someone sitting in the living room and watching television during the showing?

If you choose to allow tenants to continue to live in the property while it's in the process of being sold, make sure you're both on the same page. Ask how much time the tenants need to get the property ready for a showing, and try to consolidate showings to minimize their inconvenience. Be as clear as possible when you put this information in the listing instructions.

Another alternative is to sell once the tenants' lease ends. Make sure to understand the market before allowing your tenants to move out. You don't want to be stuck paying the mortgage on an empty property for an extended period of time if there is nobody renting! However, if your tenants aren't willing to leave during showings, this may be your only option.

ASK FOR FEEDBACK

Once a showing has ended, your agent should send a feedback request form. The appointment scheduling service that I use sends one out automatically at the end of the showing, but not everyone fills this form out.

PRO·TIP *Ask your agent to send feedback forms to buyers and to pass along any comments he or she receives. If everyone is saying the same thing, that's something you should fix.*

THEFT

One aspect of the home-selling process that isn't pleasant to talk about—but does occasionally happen—is theft. Not every person on the planet is nice, and theft may be rare, but it can happen. Sometimes thieves target open houses and houses for sale. They're looking for jewelry, electronics, and even cash, anything they can pocket easily and walk away with during showings.

Do a final walk-through of your house before leaving for a showing, and think like a criminal: Don't leave simple access to your house lying around (spare keys), and don't leave personal information on the counter (mail). Don't tempt fate. Pack up your valuables, your jewelry, your family photos, your electronics, and so on. Do not leave items at home such as laptop computers, portable electronic devices, keys to cars (any cars left at home should be locked), and anything else easily removed and valuable. Put any garage door openers inside the locked cars, or take them with you when you leave the house.

Another thief trick? Going through the home during the open house and unlocking a window or an exterior door, for easy access later. Instruct your agent to double-check everything after he or she leaves, or if you're still living in the home, double-check all the window and door locks after your agent has gone.

SELLING "AS IS"

Perhaps you don't have the time or inclination to take any of my suggestions. Maybe you need to be out in two weeks, or you're just too busy. If your home has a lot of deferred maintenance, perhaps an as-is listing is right for you. Putting language into the contract that says the property is being sold as is sets expectations so buyers know what they're getting themselves into. Homes sold as is are not in perfect condition, so buyers looking for perfection won't bother going through the home, which is good. You don't want people in the home if it's not for them.

Be careful if you choose this route because selling as is definitely has a stigma. Buyers are expecting a bargain in exchange for taking on a property that needs significant work or issues that need to be addressed. As is frequently means currently uninhabitable, so if that's not your property, then make sure to detail why the home is being sold as is. A careful explanation of the situation in the listing will go a long way toward assuaging any buyer's concerns.

In a slower market, listing your home as is can be even more of a risk. Buyers who want perfection aren't viewing it. But the buyers who are coming through are looking for an even larger discount because of the double whammy of necessary repairs in a slow market. You'll be forced to take the hit or risk losing the sale altogether, unless you have other options such as renting until the market changes.

In a hotter market, listing your home as is carries much less risk because so few homes are available. In this case, buyers will fight over just about anything.

Selling as is conveys to buyers that you won't be making repairs, which prevents them from presenting you with a laundry list of inspection issues for you to resolve.

PRO·TIP *Listing a property as is does not allow you to refrain from disclosing any material defects that you know or should know about. If you know about a broken foundation, you can't just say "as is" and skip the disclosure.*

CHAPTER 19

The Challenge of Selling Condos

Selling a condominium unit comes with its own challenges. Condos are generally less expensive than single-family homes, so they're popular with first-time home buyers. First timers generally do not have piles of money sitting around, so they turn to Federal Housing Administration (FHA) loans, which have lower credit score requirements, lower down-payment options, and so on.

Sounds like a match made in home-buyer heaven, right?

Wrong.

Condos took a huge hit during the 2008 economic downturn. Owners who had bought them with little to no money down just walked away from them in droves. Landlords who couldn't rent them out simply stopped paying the HOA dues along with the mortgages. This led to entire condo associations failing in some extreme cases. (Insert lots of new government oversight and regulations here.)

WARRANTABLE/UNWARRANTABLE

Condo associations must be approved to qualify for FHA loans—and renew their approval status every two years. If you know your condo's status is approved, you can market it as FHA approved. If your association is not FHA approved, all hope is not lost; the property can still be sold. However, the pool of potential buyers has shrunk significantly. Your buyers can pay cash for the property or apply for another type of loan.

If you're not sure whether your condo association is FHA approved—or warrantable—consider the requirements:

- Must be more than two units
- No single owner may own more than 10 percent of all units
- Must be less than 25 percent of commercial space
- Must be 51 percent or more owner occupied

The Department of Housing and Urban Development (HUD) has a website where you can search to see whether your association is FHA approved. Go to entp.hud.gov to check on your complex. You can also ask your board of directors.

HOMEOWNERS' ASSOCIATION DUES

Your condo has association dues that cover a range of services for the property. Typical services include garbage and snow removal, lawn care, general maintenance of the common areas, and a reserve fund that grows over time to pay for large-ticket items like parking lot resurfacing, boiler replacement, and new roofs.

If the reserve fund doesn't have enough money to cover the cost of these repairs, the owners may get hit with a special assessment.

SPECIAL ASSESSMENTS

HOA dues are also referred to as the assessment fee or association fee. If the HOA finds itself lacking in funds, it has the power to assess a special fee, cleverly called a special assessment.

Most commonly, the person who owns the property at the time of the special assessment is the one who pays the entire thing, although this is negotiable. If you receive notice of a pending special assessment at any time before closing, you should either plan to pay it in full or come to some sort of agreement with the buyer. If you know of a pending increase in association dues, you should also share that with your buyer.

CHAPTER 20

Why Isn't Your House Selling?

This is the part of the home-sales process that nobody wants to talk about—your home may not sell. Doing all that work to get it ready to list, deciding on a price, and leaving for every showing only to get zero offers will leave you feeling defeated and frustrated.

There are a lot of reasons a home isn't selling. Let's look at the most common ones.

PRICE

The number one reason your home isn't selling is the price. Your agent, if you're using one, should have given you a reasonable price range that similar homes in the same condition in your area are selling for.

Did you take your agent's advice?

Legally, the agent must list your home at whatever price you dictate. You are the boss of your home sale—it's your house after all! But if your price differs from what your agent recommended, don't wait too long to drop it. Ask your agent why he or she suggested the range, and look at the comps your agent is showing you.

If you did not go with your agent's initial recommendation, try reducing the price to the suggested one. If you did agree with your agent's initial price suggestion, ask for a new one. Perhaps your market has softened since the original recommendation.

Get feedback after every showing

In the last house I sold, every single person commented negatively on the cabinet handles in the kitchen. What?! This is literally the dumbest thing you can complain about, but this was a huge source of contention for everyone going through the home. (For the record, they were definitely different but not super-weird. They had been installed by the previous owner and were clearly expensive.) I made a trip to the local home improvement store and came back with $200 worth of plain vanilla cabinet handles and changed out all the others. The house sold at the very next showing. You never know what will set people off, and something you don't mind might be a *very big deal* to someone else.

Ask for feedback after every showing. Your agent should be doing this automatically. If the other agent isn't responding, ask your agent to call and get verbal feedback. Listen to what the other agents are saying, and if you hear the same thing over and over, look for ways to make a change.

Review comps again

Markets can change on a dime. If your home isn't selling, ask your agent to pull comps again. Perhaps you aren't as in line with the market as you thought you were.

Check out the competition

Ask your agent to show you other houses near you that are similar to yours—you want to know what other buyers are seeing after they're done with your house. This can also give you a great idea of what's out there, what condition it's in, and the price these other sellers feel the market will bear.

CONDITION

If price isn't the issue, is your home not selling because of its condition? A close second to price is condition. Your worn carpets just don't show as well as the neighbor's brand-new carpeting, and while your walls might not actually be dirty, a freshly painted home looks brighter and newer than one that hasn't been touched up in a few years.

Look at the small things. Are your door handles and hinges out of fashion? Is the home untidy in general? Take a good, hard look at the outside, and perhaps even ask friends to drive by and tell you their first impression. A slightly outdated home will not sell for top dollar.

Does it have an odor? This is one of the most difficult conditions to detect if you live there—and none of your friends want to acknowledge this or share it with you.

TRUE LIFE STORY

I had a client who had recently discovered she was pregnant with twins, and her two-bedroom house wasn't going to work for her family any longer. We set up an appointment to see a house just a few minutes away from hers because she loved her neighborhood and wanted to stay.

As soon as we walked into the home, we were overwhelmed by the floral scent of air freshener—so strong you could almost taste it. But not quite strong enough to cover up the fact that they had two big dogs.

Ask your best friend and your agent for their honest feedback about the scent of your home. If you get negative comments, try deep cleaning your carpets and opening the windows often to let fresh air in regularly.

CHANGING MARKETS

From 2004 to 2007, the real estate market in the United States was hot, hot, hot! Toward the end of 2007, the market stagnated, then quickly turned sour. In 2008, 2009, and even into 2010, the markets absolutely tanked in most areas, with houses going into foreclosure in record numbers. If you were buying in 2006, you couldn't possibly imagine the market of 2008, just two short years later.

Currently, 2017 is proving to be a fairly hot cycle in most U.S. markets. These markets have been rising for the past three to five years, and many are calling it a bubble. Talk to your agent about your local market, and ask whether tides are shifting.

If you find yourself in a changing market, your best bet is an aggressive approach. Lower your price, improve your home, and offer incentives to buyers such as decorating credits, buyer-specified timelines, and concessions for closing costs. A concession is either a credit or money that you give to help cover the costs usually paid for by the buyer.

If you find yourself in a changing market, revisit your why and your level of urgency. Perhaps selling right now isn't the best choice for you. Would turning the property into a rental be a better option? Can you simply remodel your home and fall in love with it all over again?

CHAPTER 21
Consider Renting

Every property has a price that will result in a sale. Sometimes this is a fair price, and sometimes it is far below what the seller needs to pay off the mortgage and other costs associated with the sale of the home. What do you do if you can't get the property sold at a price that is fair to you?

You can take it off the market, although that may not be an option for you. If you need to move, you must first sell. Or do you *have* to sell? Have you considered renting the property while waiting for a more favorable market?

There are tons of accidental landlords who never intended to rent out their property but found themselves in precisely the same position as you find yourself today.

EXPENSES

Not every property makes sense as a rental. If you paid a high price for your property yet rents are low in your area, you may lose money every month by renting it out.

Add up your monthly expenses—mortgage payment including

principal, interest, taxes, and insurance, along with any utilities you are going to pay as landlord. This is your monthly expense and basically your out-of-pocket, break-even number.

Keep in mind that this does not include any plans for vacancy or capital expenditures—big-ticket items that don't come up frequently, such as a new roof, furnace, or hot water heater. These items should be included if you have long-term rental plans.

COMPARE RENTAL PRICING

Craigslist.org is a great place to look for rental properties to gauge the market rate for your area. Go to your local Craigslist city and look for properties for rent that are similar to yours and located in or near your neighborhood. You'll get a feel for the local market rate, and you can compare the rents with your monthly expenses. This will help you determine whether renting is an idea worth pursuing.

Other websites to consider are HotPads.com and Zillow.com. (Zillow actually owns HotPads, but they function as two separate companies.) Run a search on a variety of these types of websites as though you are looking for a property exactly like the one you are selling. Compare your monthly expenses to the rent you can bring in, and determine whether you'll be able to cover your costs.

TRUE LIFE STORY

Charlie and Jenny bought a small, two-bedroom house when they first married, but they decided they had outgrown their home when they found out about their fourth baby coming. The couple started shopping for a larger home. They also thought about renting out the smaller house for some extra monthly income because they could afford another mortgage. They quickly found a tenant. Hooray!

Unfortunately, about three months into their new lives as landlords, the hot water heater broke. Charlie and Jenny aren't very handy people and had to hire someone to replace the unit. This happened on a Friday while the tenant was at work. Of course, there were extra charges for weekend repair time.

Two months later, they were again hiring someone to come to replace the broken furnace, which died in the middle of winter. Unfortunately, Charlie and Jenny did not have any reserves for these large, unplanned expenses. The cost had damaging effects on their finances.

The couple decided that after the yearlong lease was up, they would not renew their tenants, believing it would be easier to sell a vacant house. They had two months of vacancy before the property closed, adding to their losses.

How many repairs can you sustain financially? How long could you allow the property to be vacant and still make the mortgage payments? What would you do if the rental market was slow the following year? Do you have emergency contacts nearby who could shut off the water or drive by the home once you're gone? Consider these questions before diving into rental property ownership.

CONSIDER A PROPERTY MANAGER

Nobody ever gets into rental properties so they can deal with tenants and toilets. I don't know a single landlord who is excited to receive a frantic call at two thirty in the morning to hear that the furnace died or the toilet is overflowing.

If you also don't want to deal with it, you don't have to. For around 10 percent of the monthly rent, plus up to one month's rent for the initial lease signing, you can hire someone to manage your property for you.

Instead, these property managers take the phone calls in the middle of the night, coordinate all repairs, and approve tenant move-in and move-out dates. But just like real estate agents, not all property managers are the same. Start by asking for referrals from landlords you know. Drive by the properties the managers take care of to make sure they look good from the outside. If they aren't taking care of other properties, they won't take care of yours either.

Schedule a call with a property manager to see what services he or she does and does not offer. Again, ask questions until you understand the answers.

SCREEN YOUR TENANTS

The quickest way to go from happy homeowner to trapped-in-a-landlording-nightmare is to skip the tenant screening. No tenants are going to shake your hand and tell you they plan to stop making rent payments in month two. But even if they do, your mortgage company doesn't care one bit.

None of your potential clients will tell you that they deal drugs, turn tricks in their home, or have been evicted six times in the past three years either. Every single person will, without fail, make it appear that he or she is the best possible person for you to rent your property to, and a "professional tenant" can spot a new landlord a mile away.

Before you start screening, you'll want to define your rental criteria. This includes criteria like the minimum credit score you'll accept, if pets are allowed, the minimum income threshold allowed, if past evictions will be forgiven, and so on. When you decide the minimum requirements you will accept, type out your criteria and put it into a picture frame for the showings. Printing it out makes it easy to refer to during showings and makes it look like an official document rather than something you just made up on the spot, especially if the potential tenants do not meet one or more of the requirements. They'll have far less ammunition for a discrimination suit when your criteria are preprinted. Having the requirements in a frame gives people a heads-up to leave it at the property, that it isn't something for them to take with them. Also post your criteria in the listings for the rental, and when people call to request a showing, ask them for the answers. What is your credit score? What type of pets do you have? What is your monthly income?

If they don't meet your requirements, tell them, "I'm sorry, but you don't meet the requirements to rent this home. Good luck on your search." Then hang up. You want a rent check every month, not excuses for why they don't have the money.

Many potential landlords do not like this screening step and choose to skip it. Do not be tempted to just go with your gut when it comes to choosing a tenant. I have never heard of this method working out in the landlord's favor, and I spend all day, every day talking to real estate investors.

The only time you can go with your gut is when the tenant does pass the screening but you still feel that something is off. When your gut is telling you no, listen to it, and pass on the tenant. Having a vacant property for a month or two is far better than putting someone in who does not fit your criteria. The eviction process starts at one month long in the most landlord-friendly states and can be much longer. I know an investor who had to wait five years (yes, years) to get a squatter out of his property. The person didn't even have a lease with the investor; he was just squatting!

AVOID SCAMS

A common scam on Craigslist is for people to steal rental-listing images and make their own listing using your address. They charge a lower rent, accept the security deposit/first month's rent for the property, and direct tenants to have a locksmith change the locks and let them in, since the scammers are out of town. They instruct the tenants to simply deduct the locksmith charge from the next month's rent.

While you, the homeowner, wouldn't be liable for the deposit or the rent returned to the tenant, you could need to change the locks on your home and possibly even have to evict the (non)tenant from your property. There are laws that give squatters or residents rights to a property if they've lived there a certain amount of time, which is a headache you do not want.

Best to save yourself and potential tenants the hassle by simply not including the address in your listing. You should go one step further and watermark the images with your phone number so the scammers won't use them at all. Include the nearest cross streets in the listing, so potential tenants at least know the neighborhood of the property, then give out the address for showings only after you have asked the prescreening questions and received sufficient answers.

WRITE A GREAT LEASE

Your state's landlord tenant laws dictate many things you must do as a landlord, including how much notice you are required to give tenants before entering the property (you can't just go in whenever you feel like it), giving notice of nonrenewal or a rent increase, and even dictating the terms of an eviction, including documents providing notice that the tenants are being evicted.

But your state laws cover only the basics. They do not mention pets, smoking, waterbeds, or any number of other scenarios that may be important to you. This is where your lease comes in and covers your interests.

If you want your tenant to know something, spell it out in the lease. No pets? Put that language in the lease. Only pets under a specific size? Put that in the lease. Will you allow smoking in the home? I wouldn't—it's difficult to remove nicotine from the walls. A clause in the lease about late fees is helpful if your tenant is late with the rent. A clause directing that you will not accept partial rent is also a good idea. Don't expect your tenant to read minds because he or she won't. If you want your tenant to know something, spell it out in the lease.

Walk-through

Landlords can charge only for damages they can prove happened during the tenant's stay. The only way to prove this is to have a pre–

move-in walk-through, during which you document anything that is broken, stained, or otherwise damaged. You note the condition of the home on a form, and both you and the tenant sign it. Remember to give the tenant a copy for his or her records as well.

When it comes time for the tenant to move out, you can compare the state of the home after he or she has moved out to its pre–move-in condition. The security deposit should cover any damage above normal wear and tear. If you screened properly, you won't have any damage above normal wear and tear.

Check in with your tenants

You will get contact information for your tenants when they apply for your rental. After they move in and start paying rent, stay in touch with them. This tells them two things: You care about the home, and you care about keeping it in good repair. A simple e-mail or text message saying, "Hey, tenant. Just checking in to see how things are going" will be just fine.

Make repairs quickly

Tenants get extremely frustrated when they ask for a repair and it doesn't get done. Of course, you will have to make emergency repairs as soon as you can. You can't have the furnace go out in the middle of winter and wait three weeks to get it fixed. But you need to make nonemergency repairs in a timely manner as well. Do you have a handy friend or know a handyman near your property? Connect with one before you place a tenant, and call him or her when your tenant has a problem.

CHAPTER 22

Deciphering a Contract

If you're selling an owner-occupied home (not a rental property), and it's been listed on the MLS, you're probably receiving offers. Congratulations! But hold on a minute, Speed Racer. It's not time for celebrating just yet. We have much more to discuss.

All offers are not equal, and with the contract to buy and sell real estate being quite lengthy, it's easy to see the highest price on page one and automatically assume that it's the best offer.

Go back to your why—what is most important to you? Do you need the highest price? Do you need to close on, before, or even after a specific date? Do you just want to sell the home as soon as you can and be done with it?

You don't have to accept any offer. You can change your mind and decide not to sell at all, although you should read any contract before you sign it. Your agent may have you sign a contract stating that if he or she brings a ready, willing, and able buyer, you owe your agent a commission—regardless of whether the house closes. (That's pretty rare, but you should know it's a possibility.)

OFFER PRICE

The first thing you will look at is the offer price. It's on page one of every contract, and it's going to be the biggest number on the page.

Your eyes may naturally jump there, but the offer price doesn't represent final-in-your-pocket dollars.

Remember, everything is negotiable, and just because you don't like the offer price doesn't mean you should stop reading the contract. Maybe the buyers are offering something else in the contract that significantly sweetens the deal. And just as a low offer price isn't any reason to stop reading, neither is a high offer price. What are they asking you to pay farther down the page?

An offer of $205,000 with $10,000 in seller concessions is actually a worse offer than one for $200,000 with no additional requests.

You may not receive multiple offers, depending on your property, the market, and the time of year you're selling. Read through any offer thoroughly to make sure you understand exactly what it contains.

PRO·TIP   *Beware of exceptionally high offers.*

One trick I've seen in superhot seller's markets is for the buyer to make a really high offer to blow the competition away. On a property listed for $250,000, a buyer would make an offer of $275,000 or even $300,000. The sellers accept because it's so much higher than the other offers. They didn't dream they'd get that much for their home! They're so excited!

But reality slaps these sellers hard across the face when the appraisal comes back at $265,000, and now their only options are to ask the buyers to bring more money to the closing, which is not likely. You could be asking them to bring quite a bit to closing, and they probably won't have it. Remember, the bank will loan only for the price at which the property is appraised. Another option is to lower the price (best choice), or put the property back on the market, with the home doubly stigmatized by a long DOM count and a contract that fell through because of appraisal. The other buyers who made offers are long gone by the time the appraisal comes back, and our intrepid sellers are left to negotiate with only one party.

Fear not. You can still work with these high-offer buyers. Rather than accepting the offer as is, counter with a clause stating the property has to appraise only for the list price of $250,000, and any shortage will be covered by the buyers' bringing more money to the closing table.

This accomplishes two things: First, you do not have to change the status of the property while you are still negotiating the contract, so you can still continue to accept showings and potentially other offers. Second, your contract will not fall through because of appraisal, which we will discuss later but happens near the end of escrow, very close to the closing date.

EARNEST MONEY

Earnest money is a deposit the buyers give to show their interest in the property. It is typically 1 percent of the purchase price but can be very location specific, so double-check with your agent about local practices. This deposit is refundable if certain conditions—called contingencies—are not met, such as the buyer's inability to obtain financing, issues discovered during the home inspection, and even a home appraisal that does not meet the amount the buyer offered.

Earnest money prevents the buyer from tying up your property for an extended period of time and then just walking away for no reason. The buyer can still do this, but he or she forfeits the earnest money deposit, essentially paying you for your trouble. You, the seller, should not be holding on to these funds, however. Your agent, the attorney, or the title company handling the closing will hold them in a bank account specifically for earnest funds.

CONTINGENCIES

A contingency is an out for the buyers. Plain and simple, it is a way for them to walk away from the contract without losing their earnest money deposit. When reading through an offer or multiple offers, the more contingencies in the offer, the weaker it is and the greater the chance it has to fall through, no matter how high an offer price is.

Most buyers are going to need a loan to purchase your home, so a mortgage contingency is a common clause in an offer. The same for an inspection contingency—buyers want to know what they're getting into when they buy a home.

But the official contract to buy covers only so much, and buyers can ask for anything they want. Read through the contract—and any addendums—and have your agent explain anything you don't understand.

DEADLINES

In every contract, there are deadlines that must be met, or there can be consequences. For an inspection contingency deadline, if the buyer does not have an inspection before the inspection deadline, he or she can still have the house inspected—but loses the ability to walk away from the contract and receive the earnest money back because of inspection issues.

If a buyer chooses to waive a financing contingency but then cannot secure a loan—and doesn't have the cash to buy the property—he or she will forfeit the earnest deposit as well.

The dates and deadlines section of the contract should be put into your calendar and followed exactly. If you need any extensions, you should work with your agent closely and give him or her as much notice as possible to formally request an extension.

Just as the buyers cannot miss a deadline without consequence, you can't either. The only exception to this is the initial offer acceptance deadline. While it is courteous to answer the buyer by the deadline he or she requests, you are under no obligation to do so. Some buyers will put a very tight acceptance deadline into the contract to try to push you to make a decision. Their offer may not be extended if you choose to wait, but do not feel forced into choosing their deadline simply because they put it in the contract. Ask for guidance from your agent about the acceptance deadline.

The closing date is very important, as is the date and time of possession. Unless special arrangements have been made, you and all your possessions must be out of the house at the time of closing. The buyers are expecting to drive to the property after they finish signing papers so they can start moving in and setting up their new home.

TRUE LIFE STORY

When I was in eighth grade, my dad got a cross-country transfer, and we lived in a hotel for three months while my mother searched for a new house and the sale followed its course.

Customary at the time was a final walk-through of the property, then a drive to the closing office to sign the paperwork. My parents walked into the home and were shocked to discover the seller's belongings still in place—they hadn't even started packing anything!

My dad, tired of living in a hotel, told them that every day they were not out of the home, he would charge them $1,000 rent. I'm not sure whether that's legal or enforceable, but the sellers certainly got the message.

They enlisted the help of every single person they'd ever met and got everything out of that house by midnight that night.

Inspection

The inspection deadline is the date by which the inspection must be performed to allow the buyers to walk away from the contract and receive their earnest money back if necessary. It is important to note that until this day passes, the home can basically fall out of contract for any reason whatsoever, and the buyers simply exercise their right to use this contingency. An inspection does not need to have been performed to back out of the contract using this reason.

A reasonable inspection deadline is seven to ten days after the contract has been mutually accepted. Mutually accepted means all parties have signed the contract. Consider it a red flag if the buyer asks for a significantly longer inspection period without a plausible explanation.

Inspection objection

The inspection objection is the deadline by which the buyers must request any repairs or concessions based on the inspection. It may be in your best interest to try to repair these items, while the buyers may wish to just request a credit at closing for a general amount and handle the repairs themselves.

As the seller, I usually prefer to take care of the repairs myself—although when I sold my very first house, the buyers requested a repair or a $100 credit at closing. For $100, I gave them the credit and let them handle it the way they wanted.

For another home I sold, the buyers requested a simple plumbing repair—and being handy, I was all set to do it myself. They balked at the idea and requested either a huge credit at closing or having me handle it using their plumber of choice. So $125 in parts turned into a $950 plumbing bill. Ugh.

Inspection resolution

This date is typically three days after the inspection objection deadline and is a deadline that you, the seller, must meet. The buyers have written a formal request for you to give them a credit or make repairs, but that's all it is: a request.

The inspection resolution is when you either agree to their request or counter it with your own offer.

The state of your market and the reasonableness of the request should influence your decision to accept or counter. When my buyers asked for $100, that was easy to agree to. Very reasonable, and I didn't have to worry about making a repair. The state of my market actually didn't even enter my mind. The reasonableness of the request was the deciding factor.

On the other hand, the state of the market heavily influenced my decision to use the $950 plumber. I had a difficult-to-sell home in a very cool market. That $950 made sure it happened.

Financing

The financing deadline is closer to the end of the contract—around thirty to forty-five days after mutual acceptance. This is a buyers' deadline and is completely dependent on their lender. The buyers should notify you when they are approved for the loan, but they don't always follow through with this.

Put this date on your calendar, and mark it a couple of days beforehand as well. Have your agent contact the buyers' agent or the buyers to see the status of their loan approval; you can also contact them yourself, if you are selling the home yourself. In more robust markets, it isn't uncommon to need a financing approval extension, as lenders are inundated with loan requests.

Appraisal

The appraisal is required by lenders and paid for by the borrowers. The deadline for the appraisal is very close to the end of the contract. Borrowers do not want to pay for an appraisal on a home that has not yet passed inspection, so they will wait until the inspection has been resolved before ordering an appraisal.

BUYER'S LETTER

A new thing in hot markets is the buyer's letter, in which the buyers try to persuade the seller to choose their offer by including information about themselves, along with things they love about the house.

I advise my buyers to write one, and I tell them to start writing it as soon as we start working together. I tell them to pull out all the stops and use every tool in their arsenal. Military service? Better include that. Have kids? Talk about how you're looking forward to raising the kids in the home.

On the selling end, we read the buyer's letters but don't put much stock in them. I am in the business to sell my client's house to the buyer who best fits my client's needs, not the person who gives the nicest compliment about the blue kitchen or raves the most about the lovely garden. Take them with a grain of salt, and choose the best offer that fits your needs.

But perhaps you are most concerned with who is going to take the best care of your home. When you're the seller, you're the boss. Recognize that receiving a letter trying to sway you toward an offer is a possibility, and do whatever you'd like with the letter.

CHAPTER 23

Contingencies

We touched on contingencies previously—contingencies and deadlines go hand in hand—but I want to explain them in a bit more detail. Contingencies are outs for buyers, a way to walk away from the contract without financial repercussions. Buyers will put down earnest money to show their interest in a property, typically 1 percent of the purchase price.

However, buyers do not want to lose that money if the home turns out to be different than they wanted, if they can't get financing, or any other reason arises. Therefore, buyers will insert contingency clauses into the contract so they aren't bound by it should something unexpected come up.

HOME INSPECTION

A home inspection contingency means that the offer is subject to having the home inspected. While most buyers will choose a professional home inspector, this isn't a requirement. They can have a relative or friend inspect the home, or they can just inspect it themselves. The inspection contingency is a deadline by which the buyers must cancel the contract or face losing their earnest money deposit. They can still cancel the contract after the contingency deadline has passed, but they will forfeit their earnest money if they cancel because of inspection issues.

Once a home inspection has been performed, the buyer should present you with an inspection objection, a formal part of the contract in which they request repairs or concessions for things found during the inspection.

Less common is a cancellation of contract. This happens when the buyer chooses not to continue with the contract for whatever reason. I've had contracts fall out because of too many necessary repairs, standing water in the basement during the showing, and even the lack of an air-conditioning unit—even though that was clearly disclosed in the listing.

There are very few homes in which absolutely nothing is wrong. Almost all inspections will turn up something. While you wait for the buyers to make their formal request, think about what items you're willing to repair, what things you would prefer to just give a credit for, and what items are simply out of the question.

When considering an inspection objection request, keep in mind that it is only a request. Buyers may request that you have the work performed by a licensed contractor, and they can even specify a contractor they want you to use. Buyers can request a complete replacement when a repair would be sufficient. They can ask for a credit at closing or for a price reduction on the home. They can ask for just about anything they want. But it's simply a request.

You are under no obligation to comply, although you put your home on the market to sell it, and you presumably accepted their offer because it fit your needs. If you outright deny their request, they can cancel the entire contract.

Before considering the requests from the buyers, take stock of a few things: What is the state of your market? Are you in a buyer's market or a seller's market? A buyer's market puts the power back into their hands. If you really need to sell in a soft market, this may be your best opportunity.

Do you have any backup offers? If you're in a hotter market and you have someone else who has written an offer on the home, you'll need to make far fewer repairs and give far less in concessions. Keep in mind that your new buyers will most likely have their own inspection performed, and these issues may come up again.

How long has the property been under contract? Whenever a house falls out of contract, it looks bad. Unless the property falls out of contract because of the buyer's failure to secure financing, your home suddenly being relisted makes it appear like something big is wrong with it. If your home has been under contract for only a short time, your agent may be able to call up the agents of all the other buyers who went to your house and let them know personally what happened. Again, unless you're going to fix the issue, it may be a factor in every subsequent contract.

How fast do you need to sell? This all goes back to knowing your why. An urgent need for a sale should influence your decision to comply with the buyers' requests. Always keep your eye on the end result, which is getting your house sold.

Do you have your own home purchase to consider? Do you already have an accepted offer on your next home? Home buying and selling causes a chain reaction. Refusing the buyers' request can cause them to cancel the contract. If your market is soft, if you don't have a backup offer, or if you just can't get another offer before your own deadline, you could lose the next property. If you're buying in a hotter market, it may take you a long time to get another property under contract.

How strong is this contract? How strong are the buyers? Are they asking for significant price concessions or credits at closing? Do the buyers have the money to buy this house, or are they stretching themselves very thin with the purchase? Do they have a large down payment with great credit and were approved for a larger purchase? You may not want to go through the emotional back and forth of making a ton of concessions or giving up a lot of credit at closing only to discover they can't fund the deal and it all is for nothing. What will it really cost? Is their request reasonable? Are they asking for $500 to complete a $500 repair? That's pretty easy to say yes to.

Every home inspection will turn up something. No home is perfect. Even if you already had an inspection before you put the house on the market, the buyer's inspector is going to find something that needs fixing. Small items such as an outlet that doesn't work or non-GFI (ground fault interrupter) outlets near water supplies really shouldn't cause you alarm. Either have them fixed before closing or give a credit to the buyers so they can make the repairs themselves. Buyers will suggest the option they prefer when they give you a formal inspection objection.

But what happens if you have a larger issue instead of just a scary-sounding issue? Here are a few real issues to be addressed:

Asbestos

Asbestos was used in homes from the 1940s through the late 1970s as an insulator and fire retardant. Asbestos does an awesome job of insulating. However, if the fibers become disturbed and are inhaled, it can also cause mesothelioma, a really nasty cancer affecting the lining of the lungs, heart, and abdomen.

Discovering asbestos during a home inspection isn't necessarily a deal breaker. When left undisturbed, it causes no issues. Asbestos is a common pipe insulator in basements, especially in older homes. If it's intact—that is, not broken or ripped—your best course of action is usually to leave it alone. It's also good to consult an asbestos expert.

If you do find the insulation ripped or otherwise disturbed, encapsulation may be an option. Encapsulation is the process of applying a sealant to the asbestos-covered area that contains the fibers so they won't escape. (Think rubber or cement but different.) Paint is not an effective method of encapsulation, and cutting corners won't help you here.

Removal may be your only option. Unfortunately, this is extremely expensive and must be done by professionals. If you are unsure of the state of your asbestos, consult an asbestos remediation specialist before doing any work.

Methamphetamine

Methamphetamine (meth) contamination occurs when the drug is smoked or manufactured in the home at any point in time. Once your home has tested positive for the presence of meth, you must remediate it to county, state, and federal standards. This is an extremely lengthy process, must be done by professionals, and costs a significant amount of money. If your home tests positive for meth contamination, you are also required to remediate before you can sell the property. Once a property has been remediated, you may still be required to disclose the past presence of meth. Check your state laws.

Meth cannot be covered up by paint or just allowed to air out. This is a serious issue that has lasting, harmful effects to humans and pets. It is particularly harmful to children whose brains have not yet fully developed.

You would be wise to pull the home off the market during remediation. Nobody is going to make you an offer while you are remediating meth contamination. Would you want to purchase a house that way?

Radon

Radon is a colorless, odorless, and tasteless gas that can cause lung cancer. It is a naturally occurring, radioactive noble gas, and some parts of the world just happen to have a lot of radon. Other parts of the world have absolutely none.

The good news is that the presence of radon is easy and relatively inexpensive to mitigate. While every home is different, you can generally expect to pay $800 to $1,200 for a radon mitigation system.

A radon test can be performed easily: The testing equipment is placed in the lowest part of the home and sits there for a couple of days, collecting air samples. Anything above 4 pCi/L is considered high and should be mitigated. Radon levels in homes can also be reduced by adding more under-floor ventilation, sealing floors and walls, installing a radon sump system in the basement, and improving ventilation in the house overall.

Once the radon is mitigated, it is worth noting to buyers that mitigation has been performed. (Again, I believe in full disclosure of everything so that you can rest well knowing you are honest and that there is nothing that will come back to bite you after the sale.) If you live in an area of the world with lots of radon, like Mexico or parts of northern Europe, this isn't a big deal.

Wiring issues
Back in the stone age, homes were built using a variety of materials. In the 1960s, copper became so expensive that alternatives were explored. One material that gained popularity quickly was aluminum. Aluminum does not conduct electricity as well as copper and heats up faster than copper does. The repeated heating and cooling intervals make the wire droop, just enough to cause overheating.

Overheating can cause fires. Aluminum wiring had such negative connotations that it was removed from use, just as it was being improved and the threat of fire was gone.

The presence of aluminum wiring isn't always a cause for alarm, but many buyers have heard that aluminum wiring is bad and will ask for a credit at closing, ask you to repair it before closing, or worse, cancel the contract outright. Worse still, many insurance companies may not insure a home with aluminum wiring.

If you know you have aluminum wiring, yet you also know it's not dangerous, you could have an electrician certify that it is safe. But because there is such a stigma with aluminum wiring, you will most likely receive lowball offers or demands for a repair or credit before closing.

Another outdated method of electrical wiring is called knob and tube. Used from the 1880s, it started being phased out in the 1930s. It isn't grounded, so you can't use three-pronged plugs with it, and there is a fire hazard if blow-in or foam insulation is used near the wiring. Knob and tube wiring is insulated with rubber rather than plastic (as with today's wiring), and the rubber can become brittle and deteriorate with age, improper use, and poor installation techniques.

The presence of knob and tube wiring will also most likely garner lower offers or repair or credit requests.

Plumbing issues

Few issues sound as scary as plumbing problems. Visions of dollar signs and dollar bills flowing out of your wallet fill your eyes. It's best to fix a plumbing problem before it gets bad or fails completely. Find a local plumbing company and befriend it, fast.

Cast-iron outflow pipes

Back in the day, cast-iron pipes were used as outflow pipes. Cast iron is nice and strong and lasts for a really long time. Outflow pipes are just a fancy way of saying sewage pipes. All the water flowing out of your house goes through the same pipe, so the water from the sinks and showers gets mixed with water from the toilet and washing machine.

However, cast-iron pipes also rust from the inside out, and you don't really know they are about to fail until they fail. There are few warning signs of failure. If you notice a crack, contact a plumber. If your buyer's inspector notices anything other than a smooth surface, he or she will most likely suggest further inspection.

In my home, we had only one bathroom when we purchased it. Not too long after we moved in, the toilet stopped flushing and water actually went in the opposite direction! Waste started to come up into the tub, and we knew we had to unclog this thing fast. We trooped down to the basement and opened the clean-out pipe to try to see where the clog was. We stuck a pipe snake into the clean-out, poked through the last bits of rust holding the pipe together, and released a torrent of unmentionable disgusting fluid into the basement that took days to clean. Learn from my mistakes!

Leaks behind walls

Leaks behind walls are very real and easily avoidable with a good inspection.

TRUE LIFE STORY

During the last home inspection I attended, the inspector filled up a bathtub on the second floor with cold water, then took a heat-detecting gun and aimed it at the ceiling on the first floor beneath the bathroom. He let the water out, and all of a sudden, a very cold spot was detected with the heat gun. This meant that there was a leak behind the wall, and on further inspection, it was found to be significant.

My buyers were very handy and asked the sellers to have the leak repaired, but they wanted to either rebuild the bathroom themselves or choose the finish materials so they could get what they wanted.

The sellers offered a generous credit so they wouldn't have to make the repairs themselves, and the mortgage company had already performed their inspection, so the sale went through with the bathroom demolished and the leak repaired.

Broken or cracked sewer lines

Most municipalities require the homeowner to make any necessary repairs from the home to the sewer line, which is typically located in the middle of the street. Finding a crack or shift in the sewer line can be a fairly easy fix. Finding a crushed sewer line isn't as easy or cheap.

If an issue with a sewer line is discovered during the home inspection, have a sewer line repair company come out and inspect it again. Relining the pipe is far less expensive than replacing it and often does not require digging up the yard, sidewalk, or street to perform. Ask the repair company whether relining is an option.

If relining is not an option for your line, you can expect to pay thousands of dollars to have it replaced, including permits for repairing the street if necessary. You may wish to take the property off the market during the repair, if the contract is canceled. You could also offer a significant credit to the buyers to repair it themselves.

Mold
Mold exists everywhere in the world. It is literally impossible to rid your house of all mold. Also, not all mold that is black in color is black mold, the toxic, deadly mold that must be mitigated.

If mold is found during your inspection, contact a mold remediation company near you to determine how extensive the mold is and what type of mold you have.

Broken or cracked foundation
A broken foundation is not the end of the world, but it does need to be repaired and can be quite costly to do so. Contact a foundation repair company to determine the extent of the damages and get estimates for repair. If the figure isn't in your budget to make the repair, consider offering a credit at closing.

Systems issues
A furnace is required in most states. If your furnace does not work or does not work well, your buyers will most likely request a replacement. Have the furnace inspected yourself if there is any question about usability. You can expect to get between twenty and thirty years out of a brand-new furnace. An older furnace will last between thirteen and twenty years. If your furnace is nearing the end of its useful life, you may need to replace it.

Air conditioning is not required in any state. However, if you live in a warm climate and either you don't have a system or yours is not functioning, your buyers will be asking for repairs, installation, or a hefty discount.

PRO·TIP *Having a prelisting inspection can help you identify—and fix—any issues that your home has, before the buyer ever gets a chance to know about them.*

It's also important to know that when buyers make an inspection objection, it's only a request. You are under no obligation to do what they are asking. The inspection objection is subject to negotiation, just like any other part of the contract—until signed. Once both parties sign the document, negotiations have stopped, and you are now bound by those conditions in the latest version of the objection document.

Keep in mind that anything other than total acceptance of their requests can be cause for cancellation of the contract. Likewise, if your buyers make a request that seems too far-fetched, you can say no and offer to cancel the contract as well.

Be aware that having your contract fall through can give the impression that something is wrong with the house—even if the contract fell through on the buyer's side because of financing. In a cooler market, this will almost certainly stigmatize your property.

Roof issues

Whether your roof is leaking, missing shingles, or just plain worn out, roofing issues can sound scary—and costly. If your roof is completely worn out, chances are good you already know about it. But if there are just small leaks or missing shingles, you may not. When was the last time you were on the roof?

TRUE LIFE STORY

I purchased a home in the dead of winter, then sold it the following summer. Imagine my surprise when my buyers requested a new roof!

I went back to my own home inspection and read the roof section that I had apparently glossed over when it was first presented. The inspector was unable to inspect because of heavy snow. When I called him about the roof condition, he offered to come out and inspect the roof now that there was no snow cover.

He came to the same conclusion that my buyers' inspector had, that the property needed a new roof. The buyers requested a credit rather than a repair, and I was happy to give it to them rather than wait around for a roofer to be able to replace it. I was also happy to have the second opinion before I granted a credit.

Small leaks and missing shingles are not very costly repairs. In the essence of time, you may wish to offer a credit rather than actually performing a repair. Again, the amount of the credit is negotiable.

Water infiltration
If you have had water infiltration, there are most likely telltale signs. Infiltration creates stains even from the tiniest amounts of leakage, and they are very hard to get rid of.

While you are not legally obligated to disclose any issues that have been remedied, again, my personal preference and recommendation is to disclose everything anyway. The issues that have been repaired show that you are a responsible homeowner who keeps the house in good condition, and unless you've been living in a box, your neighbors know about your past house problems—and will share them with the new owners of your home.

If your buyer has water issues in the future, you could be found liable for not disclosing material defects. (Remember the water in the basement of the home that was built on the drainage lot?)

Windows and doors
Having your windows or doors fail inspection can result in a costly repair. Before you put the house on the market, you should replace any broken glass or locks. I've sold houses with windows caulked shut or that had broken hardware and would not stay open (a very old house). I disclosed these issues in the listing and specifically said the sellers

would not be addressing them, so buyers were prepared well before they ever walked in the door.

PRO·TIP *If you know of issues with your home that you do not plan on repairing, disclose, disclose, disclose.*

APPRAISAL

Before a bank will hand over a big wad of cash, they want to know that the home is worth what the buyer is paying for it.

Back before the big housing crash of 2008, banks could choose which appraiser they wanted to perform the work, or the seller or buyer could choose. As you can imagine, having a hand-picked appraiser was not the best way to determine the true value of a home, and fraudulent appraisals became more and more commonplace. As an appraiser, if you earned a reputation for messing up deals, your workload dried up.

Among the sweeping changes after the crash were appraisal rules. Buyers, sellers, and lenders can no longer choose who performs the appraisal. In fact, they can have no contact with the appraiser before the appraisal is performed.

This is both good and bad. Obviously, no one can influence an appraisal now, so you're supposedly getting a fair valuation of the home. However, the new process is a bidding system in which the job goes to the person who answers the request first—not necessarily the person with the most experience on the job or even someone who is familiar with the area.

Real estate is super-local, and what a home sells for in your area may not be the same as what it would sell for in another area. A great school district has a lot of influence on a home's value. Having an appraiser unfamiliar with the area does not help your home appraise for the full market value.

But there are some things you can do to help your cause. Here are six ways to make the most of your appraisal:

Ask whether they're local

When the appraiser calls to make the appointment, ask whether he or she is local. Real estate is local, and an appraiser from out of town may not be as familiar with the local real estate market. You want your house to be appraised relative to its location, not in relation to the local market of the appraiser from sixty miles away.

Requesting specific appraisers is no longer allowed, thanks to all those shenanigans around 2005 to 2007, but that doesn't mean you're out of luck.

"Lenders select appraisers today by sending out an e-mail blast to all appraisers on a lenders list. The appraiser who gets the appraisal is the one who hits the 'accept' button the fastest *and* who agrees to the fee the lender wants to pay. The current paradigm is: Who is the fastest and the cheapest?" says John Carlson, a California Certified General Real Estate Appraiser of JCCREA, John C. Carlson Real Estate Appraisals.

"If you get an out-of-the-area appraiser, you can try to ask for another appraiser from closer to your area," he adds, "but from what I have been told on the expert panel to which I belong, that almost never works. The lender would have to send out another e-mail blast in hopes that a local appraiser hits the accept button first."

If you do get an out-of-the-area appraiser, you'll need to be vigilant in providing data about the area. This isn't a guarantee that the appraiser will use it or even read it, but you'll want to provide a cheat sheet about the area, the comps, and any repairs or upgrades you've made.

Tidy up

You never get a second chance to make a first impression. The appraiser is going to be in your home for only a very short time—maybe an hour if you're really lucky. Remove clutter, and make the inside shine. Prepare it as you would for a showing—put everything away, and make sure the house smells nice.

This is technically not supposed to help the home appraisal. However, your appraiser is going to notice if the house is a disaster. You don't want him or her to walk into the property and have the first impression be "What a dump!" If the property is rented and you're trying to refinance, make sure the tenants know to have everything as clean as possible.

If you're selling or refinancing a property that is not tenant occupied, the only thing to do differently from what you'd do for a showing is to stay put. You want to be at the home when the appraisal is happening. You do not want to follow the appraiser around like a puppy, however, but definitely ask whether he or she needs anything, and let the appraiser know what part of the house you'll be in should any questions arise.

Look outside too

The exterior of your home should be clean and neat. If you are being appraised during grass-growing season, make sure the lawn is mowed, and clean up dead leaves and plants. If you are being appraised during snow season, make sure the driveway and walk are shoveled.

Pick up toys, trash, and debris. Do you have a dog? Remove all that evidence too. The last thing you want is for the appraiser to think your house is gross before he or she even walks in the door.

Have a list of improvements

Home appraisals are based on recently sold homes. If you've made any improvements in the property, have a list of what you've done, how much you spent, and when the improvements were made. Significant improvements on a property that was purchased recently can help the appraiser understand the scope of work and encourage a higher appraisal than the recent purchase price.

Make a cheat sheet

Measure the rooms ahead of the appraisal and have a sheet ready to give to the appraiser, who will most likely still take his or her own measurements, but having a page from you can help the appraiser make sure no rooms are missed.

Give an overview of the entire home, of course highlighting the positives. No feature is too small to mention, and some upgrades may not be readily apparent. Who can tell whether the plumbing or electrical has been upgraded by looking at the walls?

Explain the comps

Have your real estate agent pull comparable properties that have recently sold and those that are currently on the market. You should be staying on top of your local market anyway, seeing comparable properties to get a feel of what properties are selling and how much they are selling for, both before and after rehab.

Your appraiser isn't going to be able to go into the sold houses to see what they look like—he or she won't know whether the home had really cheap carpeting or stank of cats. Be prepared to give explanations of each property that has recently sold, especially those that have sold for a lower price relative to your home.

TRUE LIFE STORY

My neighbor was trying to sell her home and recently sold houses on the street had issues that weren't disclosed on the MLS. One home sold for $45,000 less than what it should have because of sewer issues. While the buyers were told of the issues before closing, those issues weren't advertised on the MLS, which is where the appraisers get their information on what has recently sold.

Another home on my street sold for $100,000 less than its true value because the prior owner died in the bathtub and went undiscovered for twelve days in the summer. That wasn't shared on the MLS either. (Note: Each state has a different way of handling death in a property. If you had a death in the home, this is an issue you need to discuss with your agent to make sure you follow proper disclosure laws.)

We typed up a sheet that played up the problem issues for each property that had recently sold and shared it with the appraiser. Her home appraised for what she needed it to, and the appraiser thanked her for the additional information.

Because comps should only be recently sold homes, any homes currently listed shouldn't be used as comps. If there is one listed significantly lower than the price you're hoping for, make sure you walk through it with your agent and understand why it's listed so much lower, and share that information with the appraiser too.

THREE WAYS TO FIGHT A LOW HOME APPRAISAL

Appraisers are human and make mistakes just as everyone else does. If your property appraises for significantly lower than what you were expecting, you may be able to challenge the results.

Double-check figures

First check to make sure the property stats are accurate. Did the appraiser include all the bedrooms and bathrooms? Is the square footage correct? Did the appraiser forget the basement or misjudge the size of the lot? If you find an error, provide evidence to the appraiser and ask that he or she reevaluate the property based on the additional information you have provided.

Know your neighborhood

Even if your appraiser is local, he or she may not be intimately familiar with your specific neighborhood. School districts can change valuation significantly. If you're located in the better school district, make sure the appraiser knows that and included that in the valuation.

Examine comparable properties

MLS listings on recently sold homes don't always tell the whole story. If you didn't share the backstory with the appraiser before and you have a low comp dragging down your home appraisal, make sure he or she understands the reason the home sold for such a low price.

Also make sure the comparable properties are actually comparable. Same neighborhood, sold recently, and so on. It's easy to mistype and get an entirely different location. Being off by even just a mile could drastically change valuation.

A traditional mortgage will not go through without a home appraisal, and if the home doesn't appraise for the purchase price, that's the end of the line. Unless you can prove that there was an error in the appraisal process, you aren't likely to sway the appraiser's mind.

Prevent this issue from happening at all by preparing all documents that portray your property in the best light ahead of time. Tell the appraiser what homes you want compared with yours by sharing a list of improvements, providing the most favorable comps, explaining the lower sales prices, and creating a home cheat sheet detailing every little thing.

MORTGAGES

Most people who are buying homes do not have a giant pile of cash sitting around waiting to purchase a home. They need to get a loan to buy your home, and if they cannot qualify for whatever reason, they do not want to lose their earnest money deposit.

Most owner-occupant contracts come with a mortgage contingency, including rates and terms that the buyer finds acceptable. If the buyers cannot find this loan within the time frame set forth in their contract, they will give you notice of cancellation or request an extension.

Not all loans are created equal. Surprise! Some loan programs have really great perks for the buyers—like low or even no down payments—but may require the sellers to cough up some cash for closing costs if the house exceeds a certain amount of money in repairs.

It's best to know these things *before* you accept an offer funded by a loan that may not be as awesome as you first think. No matter what loan program your buyer is using, always get a pre-approval letter with the offer. A pre-approval letter tells you the buyer is serious—at least serious enough to have spoken with a lender. You don't want to put your house under contract and then discover your buyer can't get approved for his or her loan. You'll waste precious days on market and have the double stigma of the house's falling out of contract.

FHA

One of the most common loan programs is called a Federal Housing Administration (FHA) loan. This loan is insured by the FHA but applied for and serviced by traditional lending institutions—meaning the Federal Housing Authority isn't giving you the loan; it's simply guaranteeing the repayment of the loan.

Since the FHA insures these loans, lenders are more willing to hand them out—they have less risk as long as they follow the guidelines set forth by the FHA.

This means that a buyer's credit score can be lower, the down payment can be less, and the buyer can still shop around for the best rates and terms. Remember, FHA doesn't issue the loan. Buyers get the loan through a traditional lender, and different lenders have different rates, different fees, and different closing costs associated with their loans.

While this all adds up to an awesome way for a less qualified person to get a loan, it isn't foolproof. The FHA loan has some quirks that affect sellers.

FHA appraisal

All properties being purchased with a mortgage will go through the appraisal process. This is not unique to the FHA process, but FHA uses its own appraisers—and just for fun, that appraisal "sticks" to the property for four months. This means that you generally cannot contest a low FHA appraisal, and any future buyers trying to use an FHA loan will be bound by this appraisal too. If it comes back less than the contracted price, you are left with very few options—either reduce the price or cancel the contract and hope for another buyer using a different type of loan, such as conventional.

Of course, if the appraisal comes back low because of inaccuracies, you should absolutely connect with the appraiser and the lender to request a review, as detailed in the previous section.

Inaccuracies include the wrong number of bedrooms or bathrooms, incorrect square footage, and omitted items like a finished basement. Basically, if the appraiser used any outdated or incorrect information that resulted in what you feel is a too-low valuation, you should request a review.

An FHA loan will also not allow property to be purchased if it's not habitable, meaning the buyer cannot live there for whatever reason, including safety, security, and structural issues. An overzealous appraiser can find too many of these items in a home and declare it uninhabitable, forcing the seller to remedy the faults or cancel the contract.

Low down payment

The FHA loan allows for a down payment as low as 3.5 percent. This is awesome for younger people or newlywed couples who are just starting out. However, coupled with a low credit score, this loan can start off on shaky ground as far as qualifying.

Any loan (except the VA loan) with a down payment of less than 20 percent comes with some form of mortgage insurance. The FHA loan mortgage insurance program is called MIP, or mortgage insurance premium. It varies, depending on the amount borrowed and the credit score of the borrower. Lesser qualified buyers with a low down payment can find themselves struggling to secure the loan.

Borderline borrowers may also do something silly close to closing and knock themselves out of a mortgage. Buying a car, charging furniture on their credit cards, and even taking a lavish vacation can disqualify them for the loan—often right around the same time the loan closes.

An FHA loan can be an excellent loan vehicle to use when just getting started or when recovering from bankruptcy or foreclosure—or simply because it has the best rate. Being aware of the limitations can help you make an informed decision when it comes time to compare apples to apples in a multiple-offer situation.

VA *loan*

The Veterans Administration (VA) loan is for military veterans, as another way of saying thank you for serving the country. A VA loan can be obtained with zero percent down for qualified borrowers, and since this loan is backed by the U.S. Department of Veterans Affairs, there is no PMI, or private mortgage insurance. This loan also comes with some of the lowest interest rates available, since the government guarantee basically eliminates risk to the lender.

A VA loan does come with a list of things the buyer cannot pay for, such as lender document fees, broker fees, transaction coordinator fees, and so on. This can present a problem for the seller—either accept these costs as part of the deal, or the deal doesn't work. One way to work around this issue is to raise the effective selling price of the home to cover the requested concessions. Of course, the property still has to appraise at the higher sales price for this to work in your favor.

There are minimum property requirements the home must meet as well. This is because the VA is lending the entire value of the home and they want to make sure the house is in the best condition possible. Among these items are a properly working heating system, water heater, and sewage system; no structural issues; and proper kitchen, bath, and living spaces. In addition, a VA loan cannot be used to purchase nonresidential space, such as an office building or a storefront.

A VA loan comes with a mandatory appraisal, as most loans do. Similar to the FHA loan, a VA loan has its own appraisers, and the VA appraisal "sticks" to the property for six months. However, the VA appraisal sticks only to VA loans, so a low VA appraisal could be scrapped, and you could sell to that same buyer with a conventional loan with no negative consequences.

A low VA appraisal can be contested by requesting a reconsideration of value. Either buyer or seller may start the process, and this gives the sale a second chance to go through.

First, read through the appraiser's report carefully. Make sure the home in the report is the same home you're selling. You don't want the appraiser to assess a three-bedroom, one-bath home when yours is actually four beds and three baths. Other areas that can get missed are the correct number of garage stalls and general square footage. If the calculations are off by just a smidge, I wouldn't worry about it, but if there is a significant difference, absolutely dispute the appraisal.

Second, double-check that the comparable properties used to value your home are actually comparable. Same bed and bath makeup, similar square footage, and so on. Have they sold recently? Three months in a red-hot market, up to six months in a more balanced market, and possibly a year in a buyer's market. Are they located within a half mile of your home if you live in a more densely populated area? Most important, if there is a big difference in school districts near you, are the comps only in the same district you're in?

USDA

The U.S. Department of Agriculture (USDA) has its own loan program, aimed at helping low-income rural and suburban families get into homes. As with any government program, there are a ton of rules to qualify for this loan program.

But with down payments as low as zero percent, the program may be worth jumping through those hoops. Check the map at https://eligibility.sc.egov.usda.gov and enter your address to see whether your property qualifies. Make sure to note in your listing whether your property is eligible for this little-known program. Many areas designated rural in the USDA loan property list have become more built up, and some surprising areas still qualify for this loan.

Use caution when accepting an offer written with a USDA loan, though. The lower the down payment, the less likely the loan will be to get funded. This isn't to say that loans with zero down are a bad thing. But borrowers who cannot save the down payment funds tend to make foolish decisions about money in general.

Conventional

A conventional loan is the one with the least amount of hassle, headaches, and "special circumstances" for borrowers. It's one of the safest options for financing a property. Borrowers need a good credit score to qualify—and borrowers with good scores are less likely to do something silly right before closing to jeopardize their purchase than borrowers with more sketchy credit.

There are no undue restrictions on the property when using a conventional loan as there are with an FHA loan—like the special FHA appraiser whose report sticks to the property for four months. If you do not like the appraisal with a conventional loan, you can just order another one. Think of it as a plain vanilla yet reliable loan program. No, it's not guaranteed, but it's a better bet.

Jumbo

A jumbo loan is just a really big loan. Conventional loans have a limit of $417,000 as of 2017, so any loan larger than $417,000 is considered a jumbo loan. It's important to note this is the loan size, not the purchase price. You can get a conforming, non-jumbo loan on a million-dollar home—if you have a down payment of $583,000.

Let's put that into a simple equation:

$1,000,000 − $583,000 = $417,000

(House price − Down payment = Loan amount)

Conforming loans have higher limits in higher-priced areas like San Francisco and New York City. For buyers to qualify for a jumbo loan, the loan payment cannot be more than 38 percent of documentable income before taxes, and the buyer must put down at least 20 percent. If you're selling a high-priced home, check the figures in the offer and discuss with your agent. For a high-wage earner, a jumbo loan is no big deal. For a regular Joe, it may be more difficult to qualify. You want to accept an offer that has the best chance of closing.

ARM

ARM stands for "adjustable rate mortgage." Adjustable rate means that the rate can change and by as mzzuch as 2 percent, in either direction.

When rates were higher, ARMs were more popular. As I write this in 2017, rates are close to historic lows and ARMs have fallen out of favor. Buyers who can qualify only for an ARM loan may not be solid buyers, so consider other factors when accepting a contract funded with this type of loan.

HOME SALE

The home sale contingency is a very common contingency in most real estate transactions. As homeowners upsize, downsize, or move across the state or country, they don't want to be left with two mortgages.

In a balanced market, you'll want to start your next home search at around the same time you put your current home on the market. If you find a house to buy before you can sell your own, your agent will insert language into your purchase contract stating you can't buy the new house until you sell your old one. Your buyers may have similar language in their contract for your house. It isn't an automatic red flag, and you can counter any clause in the contract that you wish. But be aware that the more contingencies your contract has, the more opportunities it has to fall through.

When the market is more of a seller's market, you don't have to accept this clause in your contract, and many buyers don't put it into their offer to make their offer more attractive.

In a buyer's market, you will see this in almost all offers.

What it boils down to is that if their house doesn't sell, they won't buy your house—and can exit the contract without losing their earnest money. You can lose valuable market time by accepting an offer with this contingency, and in a hot market, that can cost you thousands of dollars in reduced price or perceived issues with a home that "should have" sold quickly.

Speak with your agent about the state of your local market and whether you should be accepting an offer with this contingency.

HOME CLOSE

A home close contingency is very similar to a home sale contingency. The home still needs to sell, but with a home close contingency, the buyers have already accepted an offer on their home and are now just waiting for the process to complete.

Even in a seller's market, I would have less fear of accepting a house with a home close contingency than a home sale contingency—after all, you're probably going to be making an offer with a home close contingency too.

A home close contingency isn't guaranteed, and your agent should talk to the buyers' agent about the status of the offer on their current home—where they are in the process, how much earnest money their buyers put down, what type of loan their buyers are using, whether there were any issues that came up with the home inspection, and so on.

A home close contingency when the buyer's current home is within two to three weeks of closing, has passed inspection with a 20 percent down payment, and has a huge earnest money check for a conventional loan has a much greater chance of closing than an offer that came in yesterday for a buyer with 3.5 percent down and a check for the earnest money that hasn't cleared yet.

OFFER YOUR SURVEY TO THE BUYERS

Some loans require a survey before they will be funded. A survey is completed and provided by a survey company and should cost about $350.

After your home is under contract, you want to do everything you can to help the sale close. Many times, a survey provided by a company for a previous sale will be "reaffirmed" by the same company for a nominal fee. If you had a survey performed when you purchased the home, you may wish to offer it to the buyers to see whether their lender will accept it or whether the survey company will reaffirm. This saves them money, costs you nothing, and buys you a little goodwill.

CHAPTER 24

Moving Out

What stays in a home after you move out is typically defined as anything attached to the home in such a way that to remove it would cause damage, either to the item or the home.

Most items in the home will go with you when you move out. Things like clothing, dishes, and pillows are an easy call—they're your personal possessions. But what about appliances and furniture?

On a recent visit to a friend's new home, I noticed that a couch was built into the wall. When I asked about it, I learned that the couch came with the house (it was very distinctive). This makes sense because it was literally built into the home. If the previous owners had taken it with them, the couch would have been destroyed, or the wall would have been damaged.

But not everything is so cut-and-dried. What about the chandelier in the dining room that your parents bought you for your wedding present? Can you just take that with you? The ceiling wouldn't be ruined if you replaced the fixture. How about the shelving units in the kitchen? The hutch that you keep the dishes in?

A good rule of thumb is that if it is attached to the home, it stays when you sell. But that doesn't necessarily mean you can't take it with you. A rule of thumb is just a guideline. The best practice is to simply remove anything you can *before* the property goes on the market—so that wedding chandelier should be replaced with a different light fixture before you take listing photos or potential buyers see your home. They won't know you changed it out if they have never seen it.

If you can't change it out—perhaps you really, really want to take the refrigerator with you—direct your agent to put language into the listing stating that the item will not stay with the home. You could even go as far as posting a small note on the item stating it will not remain in the house after closing.

When in doubt, disclose. This won't necessarily stop the buyers from asking for it, but a request is just a request. You don't have to agree to it.

TRUE LIFE STORY

When I listed my last house before I got my real estate license, I specifically stated that the brand-new washer and dryer would not stay. They weren't anything special, but the neighborhood was upscale, and the washer and dryer were not. I knew they'd be replaced when the buyers moved in, and I didn't want these brand-new appliances to be tossed out.

We received an offer that included the washer and dryer, and I asked my (discount) agent to verify that the buyers actually wanted these appliances. He assured me (without calling the other agent) that if they marked them in the contract, they wanted them.

You get what you pay for with agents, and when the buyers moved in, their agent called us up, asking if we meant to leave the washer and dryer there. We had already moved out of town, so going back to pick them up was not an option. I'm sure they were tossed out when the buyers' new appliances were delivered, and I had already purchased a new set for my new home that did not come with them. Sigh.

I have read stories of sellers who have removed every light bulb in the house and every roll of toilet paper. One particularly ugly story told of a seller who dug up the garden and took the landscaping with him. Use common sense when packing up. Leave the light bulbs in place, put a new roll of toilet paper in every bathroom, and leave a roll of paper towels in the kitchen. The golden rule applies to moving out. You wouldn't want to move into a house with no TP, right?

HOW TO MOVE

Consider how you are going to leave the property once you've sold it. While nothing is absolutely guaranteed, it's a safe bet the new owners aren't expecting you to live with them.

Moving is expensive. My parents moved across the country, and it cost them $18,000. Actually, it cost my dad's company $18,000. This was for a professional moving company to come into their home, pack up all their belongings, put them into a truck, drive them across the country, and then unpack them into their new home.

And that was in 2007.

While it sounds super awesome to have a company do it all for you, your wallet may not agree. DIY is much cheaper, but then you must pack, load, and drive the truck yourself. Finding friends to help you carry boxes and furniture can be difficult, and it makes for a very long weekend. Free pizza and beer go only so far.

A hybrid solution is those moving "boxes" that look like small semi-trailers. The most common brand name is PODS, but there are several other companies such as U-Box and 1-800-PACK-RAT. The shipping container is dropped off at your house, you load it at your leisure, and then it is picked up and moved to the new location, where you unpack at your own pace. There are time limits on the rental, but they are generous. You're still moving the heavy stuff, but you don't have to drive that giant truck.

On the flip side, you can hire a company to pack your truck, and then you drive it and unpack it or hire someone at the other end to unpack for you. My husband and I did this for our last cross-country move. We didn't have any issue with driving the truck, but we knew we had too much stuff and wanted professionals to load the truck for us.

It was totally worth it too. I'm pretty sure those guys are Tetris masters.

UNPACKING

As you pack up your things in your current home, keep out items that you use frequently—think coffeepot and everything that goes with it, dishes and silverware, pots and pans.

These are the same items you will want to unpack first in your new home, along with a roll of paper towels to clean anything forgotten by the previous owners and a roll of toilet paper for each bathroom.

Add a bottle of cleaner, pillowcases, clean sheets and blankets, and towels and washcloths. Pack a suitcase with clothes, toiletries, and shoes.

Label this box or boxes as *Unpack First*—1, 2, 3, and so on. Even though I've moved more times than I can count, I still inevitably forget something necessary in my unpack-first box—and somehow manage to not mark it on the outside of any other boxes and am forced to go purchase another. (During my last move, it was the very necessary and precious pot for the coffee maker.)

CHAPTER 25
Final Steps

What happens if your buyers change their mind before closing? This is called backing out. As we discussed before, most contracts have contingencies—clauses that allow the buyers to back out of the contract and get their earnest money returned in full before a specific date.

There are rules guiding the circumstances by which they can exit the contract and receive their full funds back, but it's actually pretty easy to do, up to a certain point.

After all the deadlines have passed—or have been removed from the contract by mutual agreement—the buyers have little recourse if they choose to cancel the contract. In other words, they can't just change their minds after the deadlines have passed.

The most common course of action is called liquidated damages and means that the seller gets to keep the earnest money as both a penalty to the buyer and compensation to the seller for lost market time.

In very rare circumstances, the seller can take the buyer to court and force the buyer to continue with the purchase, but this is not common and must be specified in the contract. Most likely, your contract does not contain this clause, and it is very difficult to enforce.

Mediation is also an option, but typically mediation results in the seller's keeping the earnest money or splitting it with the buyers, depending on the circumstances under which the contract was canceled.

Before the buyers can get their earnest money returned, you must sign a release form. If you dispute the release of the funds, do not sign the form. Speak with your agent or hire an attorney for direction regarding your specific situation.

Refusing to release earnest funds for a valid reason is your right, but refusing to release them because you are angry that the buyers canceled the contract is petty and can result in a fine. Keep in mind that if you do not sign documents to cancel the initial contract, you cannot accept another contract on the property either. Read your contract to see which remedies are available.

Having a contract fall through is deflating, but dwelling on it will not change anything. Discuss with your agent and attorney your chances of winning the earnest money suit, the cost you would incur, and the time it would take. In most cases, fighting over the earnest money simply isn't worth the hassle.

TITLE INSURANCE

Title insurance is an interesting beast. It is the only insurance that insures against past events rather than future ones.

Title insurance guarantees that the person selling the property actually has the right to do so, that there are no "clouds" on the title—questions about past transfers—and that there are no outstanding liens against the property such as unpaid taxes or fines or any mechanic's liens.

A lien is a claim against the ownership of your property and is used as collateral against debt. Not every lien is bad, though. Your mortgage and any second mortgages, home equity lines of credit, home equity loans, and so on, are claims against your home that need to be paid off before the ownership can transfer to the next person. However, these are paid off at closing and are considered a normal part of the transaction.

Less common are tax liens—or liens from the county, city, state, or even federal government for unpaid taxes on the actual property, other personal property, or unpaid income tax (federal tax lien). If you have a tax lien on your property, connect with the corresponding department and work out a payment at closing or pay it off before you get to the closing table. You will not be able to sell the house with this lien unpaid.

Even less common—but unfortunately still frequent—is a mechanic's lien for unpaid work from a contractor or subcontractor who worked on a project in your home. Some unscrupulous general contractors will accept payment from the homeowner but not pass it along to their subcontractors, causing them to put a lien on your home and forcing you to pay twice for the work. If you have these types of liens on your property, it is best to find this out—and pay them off—before you put your property on the market.

A lien waiver is a piece of paper signed by the subcontractor, stating he or she has been paid in full and waives the right to place a lien on your home. You can find examples of this document online. Do not make the final payment to any contractor without this document signed!

PRO·TIP *For future reference, you should not write a check for any work on your property without a signed lien waiver from every subcontractor who performed work for you.*

This little bit of advice came to me from my dad during a huge remodel and ended up saving me more than $11,000 when I paid my general contractor the final payment only after I received a signed lien waiver from the drywall subcontractor, who subsequently was not paid by the general contractor. I felt awful for the drywall guy but was happy I knew enough to cover my backside with the lien waiver.

DEEDS
When you purchased your home, you were given a deed to the prop-

erty, which stated you were the new owner. This created the newest link in the chain of the title—a clear, traceable record of ownership of the property. Most homes have a clear title and an easily followed chain of title dating. But not all ownership transfers are smooth or even legal.

Titles can be clouded in many different ways. Before records were computerized, title transfers were recorded in a ledger book by hand, by a human being. Humans make mistakes. Numbers get transposed, tired eyes skip entire lines, and so on.

But there are also numerous nefarious ways that a title can be clouded, including outright fraud.

In one instance, a man who was divorcing his wife had a girlfriend who had obtained identification documents in his wife's name to sell the home while his wife was away. When his wife returned, she discovered the home had been sold and someone else was living in it.

In another case, two brothers inherited their father's home upon his passing. Brother Number One forged Brother Number Two's signature and sold the house without his knowledge. Only years later, after Brother Number One's death, did Brother Number Two discover what had happened.

It is common in my area for title companies to provide a "down and dirty" title search called an owners & encumbrances search, or an O&E. My local title companies will do this for a cost of $5, and it gives a very quick look at who is officially on title and what loans, if any, are outstanding. If there is a recorded mechanic's lien, back taxes, or past fines, they will show up on this report.

Ask your agent whether this is available in your area, and if it is, order one to get a quick look at your property. Any clouds on title (like human errors) can be cleared up before the property is listed, obliterating the hurdle before it becomes known and holds up a sale.

General warranty deed

The most common deed is the general warranty deed, which essentially guarantees no title defects (clouds on title) from the time that the property was first titled up until the day you sell the home.

Special warranty deed

A special warranty deed is slightly different, in that you are guaranteeing only that there are no title defects during the time you owned it up until the day of the sale.

Quit claim deed

A quit claim deed is used mainly to clear up clouds on title or transfer any ownership to another person without exchanging monetary consideration. If there was an error in the recording of a past sale or there is a divorce in which one party is buying out the other, a quit claim deed would be used.

A quit claim deed is used to literally quit any claim you may have to the property. These words are important, so let me emphasize them in a slightly different way.

A quit claim deed is used to quit *any* claim you *may* have to the property.

It does not guarantee that you have any claim to the property or that your claim is valid. To illustrate this point, I could give you a quit claim deed to the White House. I currently own zero percent of the White House and am therefore quitting my claim and handing over to you my zero percent ownership. I would not actually be conveying any portion of the White House deed to you with this quit claim deed.

You do not want to be offering or accepting a quit claim deed without legal representation and a complete understanding of what you are doing.

Bargain and sale deed

The bargain and sale deed is used mostly for the sale of court-seized residential property. It conveys title from seller to buyer but does not guarantee that the seller owns the property free and clear. It is similar to the quit claim deed, except the property is being sold rather than transferred.

TITLE INSURANCE TO THE RESCUE

With title insurance being required by lenders, and the computerization of land records, there are still surprises, but they're far fewer than in years past. Your title insurance policy will give you a list of items it will not insure against, called exceptions to the policy.

As the seller, you will choose the title company, and in states that do not typically use an attorney for closing, you will sign all the paperwork at the title office. There is a line on the standard purchase and sale agreement that gives the buyer the option of having the seller choose and pay for the title costs or having the buyer choose and pay.

One trick that some buyer's agents use is to check the box that says buyer chooses and pays, then writes up an addendum that states the buyer chooses XYZ Title and the seller pays.

Remember, you can counter anything. The most important thing in choosing a title company is to use a large, national company that has been in business for a considerable amount of time. Reputation and experience are very important when issuing title insurance.

TRUE LIFE STORY

I take a lot of continuing education courses as a real estate agent. One course, titled Four Cases of Fraud, told of a title company that did not secure its wire transfer properly. Closing happened as normal, the buyers gave their money, and the title company received it. The title company sent a wire to the seller's bank to pay off the mortgage, but it was somehow intercepted or rerouted. The seller didn't know anything was wrong until he received notice a few months later that the bank was going to foreclose on the original property.

The title company, a local, independent operation, could not afford to repay the stolen money and simply closed up shop. The resolution is pending.

CHAPTER 26

At the Closing Table

You've made it to closing!

The first step is possession. In the typical selling process, the buyer takes possession at closing, meaning the seller must have all his or her belongings out of the home when signing papers to transfer ownership. Any other scenario must be mutually agreed on in the contract.

If the buyer wants to move in early, you must agree to this in writing.

If I were your agent, I would not recommend agreeing to this situation. Any number of things can go wrong in the days leading up to a home sale. The sale could also not go through! The buyers could also use the opportunity to find any and all things wrong with the home and delay or threaten to cancel the closing unless you repair them. While it is tempting to agree to this arrangement so the sale does not fall through, it is in your best interest to say no. There is almost no upside for you as the seller and way too much downside.

On the other hand, if you want to stay in the home after you sell it, you must have the buyers agree to it in writing. This is called a post-closing occupancy agreement. You may have to negotiate some form of remuneration for your time at the home, but this generally can be worked out with the buyers. They do not owe you this, and since it deviates from the normal process, you may wish to have a backup plan in case they do not agree.

Whether you are giving up possession at closing or continuing to live in the property for an extended period of time following the sale, when you do ultimately relinquish possession, you should give your buyers a home that is clean, swept, and vacuumed, with all trash out of the home.

CLOSING

You are going to have a lot of expenses at the closing table. With so many different cities, counties, and states in America, it is impossible to cover every scenario. A rough estimate for closing costs is 2–4 percent of the purchase price, not including the agent commission. Ask your agent for a more tailored estimate, including any transfer tax, which is a fee to transfer ownership to the buyer. (Not all states have this.)

Also ask your closing agent what you should take with you to closing. If you are surrendering possession at closing, you'll need to bring all the keys to the house, all the garage door openers, any combinations or codes for locks or keypads that are staying with the house, and personal identification such as a driver's license to prove who you are. Double-check with the closing agent regarding documentation; some require more than one form of identification.

In addition to the agent's commission, there are a lot of small and not-so-small fees that you are responsible for. Let's look at some of these fees so the sticker shock is considerably less.

Prepaid taxes

Most municipalities bill for taxes in arrears, meaning the bill you receive in April is for last year's taxes. You are responsible for paying the taxes for the time you live in the home, and the time is calculated to 11:59 the night of closing.

If your tax bill for the previous year has arrived, it will be paid out of the seller's funds at closing. If your tax bill has not yet arrived, you will be charged a certain amount of money—specified in the purchase agreement—to be put into escrow for the new owner to use to pay the taxes once the bill arrives.

You will also be charged for the year-to-date taxes that have not yet been assessed; again, the purchase contract will dictate how much you will owe, and it will also be held in the buyer's escrow account until it is due.

Final water bill

In many states, a set dollar amount for the last water bill will be withheld from your closing proceeds until the final bill is sent to the title company, should one not be available on the day of closing. The title company will pay it from the escrowed proceeds and will send you the remainder of the funds it withheld.

HOA statement letter

If your property is located in an HOA community, you will be required to provide a letter from the HOA management company stating your account is paid and current. You may also be required to provide a letter from the management company attesting to the current HOA dues, any special assessments, fines, fees, and so on. Conveniently, this letter is available for a fee. My own letter cost something like $125, just to say that I had no late balance and to confirm the HOA dues.

Credits or concessions

During the offer negotiation, your buyer may have requested concessions or asked you to pay for items typically covered by the buyer. Anything you agreed to, such as a certain dollar amount to help with closing costs, will appear on the closing statement as a debit on the seller side and a credit on the buyer side. Double-check these figures, and if you see an error, notify your closing agent immediately.

HUD statement

The settlement statement, or HUD-1, is the listing of all the debits and credits involved in the sale of your home. You may be thinking that if you sell for $200,000 and you owe only $100,000, you will be taking away a check for $100,000. In 2015, the way that closings were handled changed. If you bought your house before 2015, your closing went differently from how it will now.

On the seller side, the most important part of the changes to the closing process is the closing date. Actually, it's the lender-disclosure-to-the-buyer date, which must happen three business days before closing. This is pretty much set in stone unless you, the seller, are facing imminent foreclosure or similar dire consequences. If the lender makes a mistake, or circumstances change within three days before closing, the lender must provide a new document to the buyers and must give them three days to review these documents, effectively pushing back your closing date.

Keep in mind that if your buyers request an amendment to the closing date, it is much easier to comply with the request than to find a new buyer altogether.

Cashier's check fraud

In years past, the buyers could have their bank wire their portion of the purchase price—the total mortgage they are taking out—and they would bring a cashier's check for the down payment to the closing table. But cashier's checks are easily forged, and bad checks cost the title companies too much money. Most title companies have reduced the dollar amount they will accept in cashier's check form; some go as low as $1,000.

TRUE LIFE STORY

When I sold a house recently, this policy was in effect at the title company that my buyers were using. As I have bought and sold numerous houses, I didn't really read through the instructions I received from the closing agent. I won't ever make that mistake again!

The afternoon before closing, I received a phone call from the closing agent, asking where my funding was. I assumed she was talking about the lender and offered to call to double-check they had sent their wire.

She replied, "No. I've received the lender wire. I'm looking for the buyer's wire."

"My buyers are bringing a cashier's check with them for their down payment," I told her. Imagine my surprise when she told me that they no longer accept cashier's checks for down payments, that my buyers had to wire their portion of the purchase price, and that by the way, wire deadlines were almost up.

Thankfully, we were able to make the wire happen, and the sale went through, but I spent a very frantic hour or so working to get that wire transfer completed.

This is as much a caution for you, the seller, as for when you turn around and buy your next home. Again, it's easier to push the closing date back by one day than to find a new buyer altogether. You'll close faster too.

WIRE FRAUD

So, if cashier's checks can't be used, how do you buy a house? Enter the wire transfer. Safe, secure, and instant. Sort of.

The wire transfer is safe and secure, as long as you are sending the money to the correct account. It is instant, in that the moment you send the wire, the money is out of your account. It can take a few hours to appear at the other end.

But the wire transfer is not perfect.

My friend was buying her first house. She scrimped and saved and managed to put together a down payment of 20 percent—to the tune of more than $52,000.

She found a house, had her offer accepted, and started her communications with the title company. She soon discovered that it was slow to respond and slow to give her information. The afternoon before the closing, the title company sent her the wire instructions and told her she couldn't use a cashier's check.

Her frustration levels were running high, and she made plans to have the funds wired the next day. Overnight, she received another e-mail from the title company, giving her new wire instructions and apologizing for sending the wrong bank account information.

She thought she was lucky to have checked her e-mail that morning and gotten the new instructions. It turns out the title company's e-mail had been hacked, and a scam artist had sent her its own bank account information.

She went from excited to devastated in a heartbeat. Her money was gone.

To make matters even worse, after she notified the title company of what had happened, it disclosed that this had happened before. In fact, it had happened at least 30 times in 2017!

Yet she was not warned this could happen, was not given wire instructions during her initial communication with the title company, and was told they would not change, not given any indication that there was even a problem.

But this story has a happy ending! She was scammed by possibly the dumbest criminal on the planet, who rerouted the money from her account into his own U.S. bank account and then left it there long enough for the scam to be discovered. My friend made a claim with her bank immediately, and the stolen money was held by the scammer's bank until the truth could be determined.

Smarter criminals take the money from you, then whisk it away to a foreign bank, where it is lost forever.

I've heard of this scam before, and it happens on both the buy and sell side.

As the seller, you will be receiving a large sum of money from your buyer. You in turn will most likely be sending this large sum via wire transfer to the bank that currently holds your mortgage. If the wire is not received, you are still on the hook for the mortgage.

Avoid the scenario above by taking the utmost precautions. Call your current lender, using a phone number printed on the mortgage documents. Ask for a payoff amount and wire instructions. Ask the lender to confirm that these instructions will not change between now and closing.

Give these instructions to the title company. If you are living in your home, chances are good the title company is nearby. Consider driving the instructions over to the title company so you know it received the right bank account information and you know your money is safe, your mortgage is paid off, and all is right with the world.

I recommend you choose the title company, pay your portion of the closing costs associated with title, and go with the big guys unless the buyer insists on using a different company—and pays the entire bill. The national title companies that have been in business for decades with great reputations have procedures in place to help avoid these issues, and it is standard operating procedure to verbally double-check wire instructions before sending.

Also, make it your standard operating procedure to verbally verify the wire transfer information—if you're not hand-delivering it—before you pass it along to the lender or title company. There's just too much at stake.

ATTENDING CLOSING

As the seller of the property, you do not need to be present when the buyers sign their documents. Indeed, you will discover that the seller side of things is noticeably shorter than the buyer side. Closing agents explain all documents to the party who is required to sign them, and the buyer signs significantly more paperwork than you do as the seller. While you as the seller are certainly allowed to be there, you also have the option of signing early.

The sale is not complete—and you do not get your money—until the buyers sign all their paperwork and their loan is funded. But if closing doesn't fit into your schedule, you can make arrangements with your closing agent to sign ahead of time. The closing agent will wire your funds to you after closing, or you can choose to pick up a physical check. In fact, most closing companies now charge a fee for the actual check, while wire transfer is typically free.

If you're interested in skipping the closing, talk to your agent and title company to see whether this is an option for you.

CHAPTER 27
Sold

Congratulations on your sale! That was fun, wasn't it?

Well, the actual move probably wasn't fun. Hopefully you packed properly and nothing broke! One last tip for you: Unpack everything within the first month of moving in. Really go through things as you put them away, and if it's been a while since you packed that box, perhaps you have realized you don't really need what's inside after all.

Offer your boxes to someone else on Craigslist.org once you're done with them. People are always looking for moving boxes.

Let's review the things you'll need to do to sell your home.

1. **Figure out your *why* for moving.**

2. **Determine how urgent your need to sell is.** Don't skip these first two steps! These are very important when it comes to reviewing offers later on, especially if you receive a low offer or multiple offers.

3. **Get the house ready to show.**

4. **Declutter.** These steps take the most amount of time. You're making repairs and removing items you don't need, and it can be difficult to pack things away. Once you've made any repairs or upgrades, it's time to get rid of all the extra stuff you have lying around. Refer to your why and your urgency for extra boosts of determination.

5. **Improve your curb appeal.** You want buyers to love your home the minute they drive up.

6. **Gather documentation.** Any paperwork related to your home should be saved for the new owner: copies of permits for any work done, information for anything still under warranty, owner's manuals for appliances, and so on. Gather these items up and put them aside for the new owner so you don't accidentally pack them.

7. **Determine how you'll list your house.** Full-service agent? Flat-fee agent? Or FSBO?

8. **If you're using an agent, start interviewing.** You want to find a great agent, not just the first person to offer his or her service.

9. **Determine your asking price.** What can your home realistically bring in?

10. **Take good photos of your home.** DIY or hire a professional. You need great images that accurately portray your home.

11. **Review your listing.** Once your house is listed in the MLS, review the listing for accuracy.

12. **Be prepared for showings at any time!** This means preparing to leave your house at any time.

13. **Market your property.** It's more than just word of mouth!

14. **Go under contract.** Review all offers and negotiate the price until you are satisfied.

15. **Prepare for a home inspection.** What needs repairs? How much will they cost?

16. **Finalize an inspection resolution.** What are you willing to fix or provide a credit for?

17. **Get ready for an appraisal.** Make sure the appraiser knows the local market.

18. **Pack the rest of your things.**

19. **Move out.**

20. **Close.**

Good luck! You can do this. I believe in you. Let's get started selling.

Acknowledgments

This book would not exist without the encouragement from Brandon Turner, the direction from Katie Askew, the wisdom of Scott Trench, and the company that brought us all together, BiggerPockets.com.

I should throw Josh Dorkin in there because he started BiggerPockets. Without him, none of us would know each other.

Also, thank you to Morgan Housel, who put this whole ball into motion. Thank you to my copy editor, Paul Silverman, and proofreader, Michael Lavrisha, for fixing my grammatical errors. Thank you to Craig Curelop and Evan Miller for being my first readers.

More from
BiggerPockets Publishing

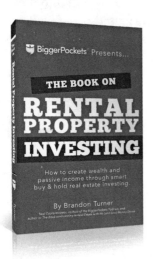

The Book on Rental Property Investing
The Book on Rental Property Investing, written by Brandon Turner, a real estate investor and cohost of the BiggerPockets podcast, contains nearly 400 pages of in-depth advice and strategies for building wealth through rental properties. You'll learn how to build an achievable plan, find incredible deals, pay for your rentals, and much more! If you've ever thought of using rental properties to build wealth or obtain financial freedom, this book is for you.

The Book on Investing in Real Estate with No (and Low) Money Down
Lack of money holding you back from real estate success? It doesn't have to! In this groundbreaking book from Brandon Turner, author of *The Book on Rental Property Investing,* you'll discover numerous strategies investors can use to buy real estate using other people's money. You'll learn the top strategies that savvy investors are using to buy, rent, flip, or wholesale properties at scale!

If you enjoyed this book, we hope you'll take a moment to check out some of the other great material BiggerPockets offers. BiggerPockets is the real estate investing social network, marketplace, and information hub, designed to help make you a smarter real estate investor through podcasts, books, blog posts, videos, forums, and more. Sign up today—it's free! **Visit www.BiggerPockets.com.**

The Book on Tax Strategies for the Savvy Real Estate Investor

Taxes! Boring and irritating, right? Perhaps. But if you want to succeed in real estate, your tax strategy will play a huge role in how fast you grow. A great tax strategy can save you thousands of dollars a year. A bad strategy could land you in legal trouble. That's why BiggerPockets is excited to introduce *The Book on Tax Strategies for the Savvy Real Estate Investor*! You'll find ways to deduct more, invest smarter, and pay far less to the IRS!

Set for Life: Dominate Life, Money, and the American Dream

Looking for a plan to achieve financial freedom in just five to ten years? *Set for Life* is a detailed fiscal plan targeted at the median-income earner starting with few or no assets. It will walk you through three stages of finance, guiding you to your first $25,000 in tangible net worth, then to your first $100,000, and then to financial freedom. *Set for Life* will teach you how to build a lifestyle, career, and investment portfolio capable of supporting financial freedom to let you live the life of your dreams.

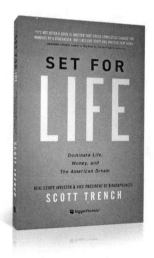